THE WALTER LYNWOOD FLEMING
LECTURES IN SOUTHERN HISTORY

LOUISIANA STATE UNIVERSITY

OTHER PUBLISHED LECTURES IN THIS SERIES:

The
Texas
Revolution

By
William C. Binkley

★

LOUISIANA STATE UNIVERSITY PRESS
Baton Rouge

MANUFACTURED IN THE UNITED STATES OF AMERICA
BY THE VAIL-BALLOU PRESS, INC., BINGHAMTON, N. Y.

PREFACE

IN THE PREFACE to his two-volume collection of *Official Correspondence of the Texan Revolution* (New York, 1936), published under the auspices of the Albert J. Beveridge Memorial Fund of the American Historical Association, the present writer stated that the history of the Texas Revolution had not been written and that until a number of detailed studies of various phases of the struggle could be made, "it would perhaps be unreasonable to expect an adequate synthesis." Fifteen years later the picture remains essentially the same. Although a few brief articles have thrown new light on some of the incidents or individuals involved, the comprehensive story of the movement as a whole is still waiting to be told; and much work remains to be done before it can be told. The four lectures which constitute this little volume make no pretense, therefore, of presenting a history of the revolution. They do not attempt to describe the work of the successive provisional governments which undertook to direct its course, for example; nor do they follow the intricacies of the military operations or the complexities of such problems as finance or diplomacy. Instead, they should be considered as an interpretative study, based on what is known about those activities, in which an effort is made to examine the salient features of the struggle with only such supporting detail as seems necessary to explain their development and to indicate their significance.

These lectures were delivered at Louisiana State University in May, 1950, as the Thirteenth Series of the Walter Lynwood Fleming Lectures in Southern History, and they are being published here without material alteration in form and content. They are the product of more than a quarter of a century of interest in the Anglo-American activities in Texas before annexation, and they are based upon an intensive study of most of the available contemporary material which seems to have a bearing on the subject. The most important collections of official materials, both manuscript and published, have been described elsewhere (see *Official Correspondence of the Texan Revolution,* xi-xxi), and to these should be added the enormous store of personal papers in the University of Texas Library and other personal collections in depositories scattered across the country from the New

York Public Library to the Bancroft Library of the University of California. Since the format of the series does not provide for footnotes and bibliography, it has not been possible to cite the sources from which quotations and other specific information have been drawn, but it should not be difficult for the trained investigator to locate them.

My indebtedness to the scholarly work of Professor Eugene C. Barker—especially his *Life of Stephen F. Austin* (Nashville, 1925), and his *Mexico and Texas, 1821–1835* (Dallas, 1928)—will be obvious to every serious student of Texas history. Special mention should also be made of Harbert Davenport's "The Men of Goliad," *Southwestern Historical Quarterly*, XLIII (1939), 1–41, which has provided the basis for some of the generalizations in the last two of these lectures. The Southern Historical Association has generously permitted me to incorporate into the fourth lecture portions of my article on "The Activities of the Texan Revolutionary Army after San Jacinto," which appeared in the *Journal of Southern History* in August, 1940 (VI, 331–46). I am also grateful to the American Historical Association for permission to include in the fourth lecture several paragraphs from the introductory essay which I wrote for the *Official Correspondence of the Texan Revolu-*

tion, mentioned previously (compare especially pages 107–108, 118–19, 120–27, with pages xxv–xxvi, xxx–xxxi, xxxiii–xxxvi, of the Introduction).

The final stages of the research work and the writing of these lectures were made possible by a grant-in-aid from the Social Science Research Council for 1949–50, supplemented by a similar grant for the summer of 1949 from the Carnegie Foundation Research Program administered by the University Center Research Council, representing Vanderbilt University, Peabody College, and Scarritt College.

WILLIAM C. BINKLEY

Vanderbilt University
January 31, 1951

TABLE OF CONTENTS

I

CONDITIONS IN TEXAS ON THE EVE OF THE REVOLUTION

THIS SET of lectures ought to begin, perhaps, with a philosophical consideration of the role which revolutions have played in making the present what it is; but when we find the term being applied more or less indiscriminately to events as different in character as a presidential election on the one hand and a gradual change in industrial methods over approximately two centuries on the other, it seems clear that we do not yet have an adequate basis for sound generalizations. Obviously, many of the movements which we now loosely call revolutions need to be studied more carefully before we can expect to reach dependable conclusions concerning the meaning of revolutions in general. With the hope of making a small contribution toward the attainment of the ultimate goal, therefore, these lectures will undertake to examine and explain the struggle by which a group of Anglo-Americans in Texas gained their independence from Mexican rule in 1836. Although much has been written about the Texas Revolution, it is still being misunderstood and misinterpreted in standard historical works. It has been described variously as a part of a deliberate design of the South to extend the slave territory of the United States, as a plot of speculators to enhance the value of their investments, and as a spontaneous uprising of outraged freemen against the threat of tyrannical oppression. On the other hand, any serious study of the vast amount of contemporary material which has a bearing upon the subject seems to lead to the conclusion that none of these characterizations can be accepted as accurate. But before we can undertake to say what the Texas Revolution was, we must try to see something of the circumstances out of which it developed.

The details of the general background need not concern us here, but certain salient points must be hastily reviewed. We know that in 1821 Anglo-American frontiersmen, pressed by the combination of the panic of 1819 and the termination of the credit system in the disposal of public lands in the United States, began to seek new economic opportunity in Texas, where the Spanish authorities were showing signs of a more liberal attitude toward foreigners. We know also that in that same year the Mexican subjects of Spain established their independence and began the arduous task of transforming the former Spanish viceroyalty into a federal republic. In a penetrating analysis of the train of events which stemmed from these two concurrent developments, Professor Eugene C. Barker has shown that the basic factor was the difference in the background of the two groups of people who thus came into contact with each other on Mexican soil. On the one side was the influence of the Anglo-American frontier experience, which had promoted a spirit of resourcefulness and self-reliance and had provided for a practical application of their democratic theories of government and individual liberty as the pioneers had moved westward on their own responsibility. On the other side was the effect of nearly three centuries of autocratic Spanish rule, which had left little room for the acquiring of political wisdom or the development of initiative and resourcefulness as the Mexican frontier had been advanced northward by official propulsion. "With the political ascendancy of the two elements reversed," says Barker, "the situation would have held no threatening aspects, but with the Mexicans in the political saddle conflict was certain."

[3]

In adopting the federal constitution of 1824 the Mexicans provided themselves with a complex system of government which was beyond their capacity to understand or administer, and in their stumbling efforts to follow its provisions they soon became involved in political confusion. Factional strife was so intense that only the first president was able to serve out the term for which he was elected, and in one four-year term the office changed hands four times. Because the official actions sometimes impinged upon rights or privileges which the Anglo-Americans considered to be guaranteed under a federal system, minor misunderstandings inevitably developed. In its enumeration of the states which it was bringing into existence to form a federal union, the constitution arbitrarily joined Texas with the neighboring province of Coahuila, and the national congress then instructed this artificial state to work out its own program of local government. With only one representative in the legislature, the Anglo-Americans were clearly at the mercy of the Mexican majority; but, in general, the authorities were so preoccupied with their own quarrels that they neglected either to provide for the needs or to enforce the regulations incident to the colonization of Texas. Under the guidance of Stephen F. Austin the settlers managed for a time to avoid becoming involved in the domestic upheavals, but their ability to remain aloof was compromised when the repeated efforts of the United States to purchase Texas led the Mexican authorities to suspect that the influx of colonists was part of an organized scheme to despoil Mexico of territory. By 1830, therefore, they were determined to take issue with their Anglo-American subjects.

Three problems which had already caused the colonists some concern were the requirement that all settlers in Texas must be Catholics, the recurring indications of Mexican opposition to slavery, and the failure to make adequate provision for the machinery of local government through which they might have a direct voice in the administering of their own affairs and the maintaining of order. Thus far, however, the authorities had shown little disposition to raise any question concerning the religious affiliation of the immigrants; and on the question of slavery, prohibitory measures which had been adopted by both the state and the national governments were virtually nullified when Mexican officials collaborated with the colonists in working out a system of contract labor which permitted its continuation in fact if not in name. But in both cases the continued existence of the restrictions constituted a potential danger that could not be ignored. The third problem, on the other hand, grew out of a need for positive action. In their efforts to obtain a more adequate system of local administration the Anglo-Americans were simply following the precedents of earlier frontier experience in the United States, but the suspicious Mexican mind construed their requests as evidence of a plot to undermine Mexican institutions, instigated no doubt by the aggressive neighbor to the north. The response was the passage of the famous law of April 6, 1830, which placed a ban on further immigration into Texas from the United States and provided for the garrisoning of the province with convict soldiers to ensure the enforcement of Mexican laws.

To the Texans the adoption of these provisions indicated that the period of easy indifference on the part of Mexican authorities was about to be superseded by regulation and enforcement. Although they strongly resented the sudden change from neglect to a policy of control, they accepted Austin's conservative counsel to refrain from demonstrations while he attempted to obtain the suspension of the most objectionable features of the law. As usual, however, the Mexican's enthusiasm for enunciating principles was tempered by his incapacity in trying to apply them, and in the end neither of the general aims of the law was carried out as planned. Efforts to put the military plan into operation were thwarted in large part by the particularistic attitudes of the state governments, and the few troops that got to Texas served to irritate rather than intimidate the colonists until the overthrow of the authorities who had sent them forced their withdrawal. Austin succeeded in obtaining an interpretation of the ban on immigration which left the door open for a diminished flow on an authorized basis, while in the absence of an effective military force many others continued to come without authorization. For the time being the plans for more rigid control obviously had failed, but the new legislation remained on the statute books. The net result was to increase the apprehension of the Texans concerning their status under Mexican rule and to strengthen their conviction that if the authorities would permit them to work out their own solutions for their problems, much of the cause for friction could be removed.

There were no outward signs of active resistance, however, until 1832, when the federal soldiers stopped the work of state land surveyors and attempted to collect tariff duties from which the colonists had hitherto been exempt. Incensed by these and other arbitrary acts of the Mexican commander at Anahuac, on Galveston Bay, the Texans made an

organized attack on the post, and their success precipitated the departure of the troops which had been
sent to the province in 1830. On discovering that this
action had coincided with a new upheaval in Mexico
directed against the authorities who had sent the
troops, the Texans adroitly explained that they had
acted to protect themselves from the repeated "encroachments and infractions which have been made
by the present administration upon the constitution
and laws of our adopted and beloved country." This
explanation was accepted by Antonio López de Santa
Anna, the leader of the new uprising, as evidence of
their adherence to his cause; and as they watched the
successful progress of his revolution they began to see
prospects of more satisfactory relations with the
national authorities. Hoping to profit from the liberal
principles which he was supposed to represent, they
resorted to the traditional Anglo-American frontier
procedure of calling a convention through which they
might petition for reforms in the handling of their
affairs.

Representatives from every important community
in Texas, with the single exception of San Antonio,
assembled at San Felipe in October, 1832, in response
to this call. Committees were appointed to draft
memorials asking for the repeal of the ban on immi-

gration, for a reduction of the tariff and the regulation of customs officials, for a more efficient organization of local government in order to remove confusion in issuing land titles and to facilitate the administration of justice, for permission to organize their own militia to provide protection against Indian depredations, and for the separation of Texas from Coahuila and admission to statehood "on an equal footing with any of the states of the Union." These memorials were not presented to the Mexican authorities until they had been reconsidered and reaffirmed by a second convention, held in April, 1833, in which the additional step was taken of drafting a constitution for the proposed new state. Stephen F. Austin, who had undoubtedly done more than any other individual in Texas to maintain peaceful relations in the past, was selected to carry the petitions to Mexico City, where Santa Anna had just succeeded to the presidency.

Austin left Texas full of confidence for the success of his mission, but on his arrival at the capital he found that Santa Anna was absent on a military campaign to crush the last vestiges of the preceding regime. In trying to deal with the acting president, he discovered that the professed zeal for liberal reform was more theory than fact and that the proposals which had looked so fair in Texas bore a different aspect to the Mexican authorities. In fact the very method by which these proposals had been prepared and presented was sure to be misunderstood in Mexico, where long-established precedent decreed that any requests from the people should pass through the channels of a hierarchy of officials from the alcalde, or local magistrate, to the supreme national authority. After six months of almost unceasing effort to allay suspicion and to show the honesty of the motives behind the requests of the Texans, however, Austin was finally informed that the law prohibiting immigration from the United States had been repealed, that the request for separate statehood had been denied, that the petitions concerning tariff adjustments had been referred to the treasury department, and that all those relating to local administration had been sent to the authorities of the state of Coahuila-Texas with recommendations for favorable action.

Believing that he had accomplished all that was possible for the time being, he began his homeward journey in December, only to be arrested by order of the acting president in January, 1834, because of a letter which he had written three months earlier urging the local authorities at San Antonio to cooperate with the Anglo-Americans in their efforts to set up a state government. He was taken back to

Mexico City, where he was forced to remain in prison from February until December, 1834, while court after court disclaimed jurisdiction over his case. Finally, after intercession by loyal Texans, he was released on bail but required to stay in the city until July, 1835. During these eighteen months he had ample time for reflection upon the relations between Mexico and the Texans, and while his correspondence of the period always urged a spirit of moderation, the result of this experience was to become manifest after he had regained his complete freedom.

Meanwhile the situation in Texas itself was not entirely satisfactory. During the period when Austin was working to obtain action on their petitions the colonists remained quiet. But when they learned early in 1834 of the rejection of their request for separate statehood and of Austin's arrest, they faced a dilemma. There was a fear that a failure to protest might be construed by the Mexican officials as acquiescence in all that had been done, but on the other hand any organized effort to oppose the government's policy might endanger Austin's chances of immunity. Perhaps the best evidence of their lack of hostile intentions was the fact that these new developments found them without a positive plan of action. But future relations would be influenced to a large extent by the attitude of the authorities toward questions affecting local interests, characteristics, and progress. Hence a consideration of the general conditions in Texas about 1834 is essential at this point.

Viewed as a phase of the westward movement of the Anglo-American people, the settlement of Texas had come to the transitional stage between two generations of frontier development by the beginning of 1834. For approximately twelve years the guiding genius of Austin had determined the nature of its progress, and under his influence a new society, manufactured out of raw material and personnel, had been planted on Mexican soil. The first comers had migrated to make better conditions for themselves, and they were willing to stake their hardihood and fortune against the uncertainties involved in a change of their national allegiance. The success of their venture seemed to remove much of the element of chance, with the result that a steadily increasing stream of immigrants poured into the region with a force that could not be dammed by Mexican legislation. The typical life had been that of the frontier farmer clearing his fields and building his home. But with the growth of the population the individual or family need was now ready to be merged into the group interests, and attention had to be turned to the establishment of the institutions of a stable society. The school and the church, local government and protective organization, must be developed; and the transition from primitive agriculture for domestic purposes to convertible husbandry as a basis for commerce and industry must be fostered. That the Texans realized that such a change was taking place was indicated by their efforts to obtain from the central government of the Mexican republic a more careful and intelligent consideration of their needs. The conventions of 1832 and 1833 were in a large measure reincarnations of similar action on earlier Anglo-American frontiers all the way from Watauga to Missouri, but in this case the appeals were being made to authorities who possessed only the faintest conception of their real significance.

As a basis for determining the population and the general economic conditions in Texas during this important period of transition it is necessary to depend largely upon reports made at the time by two individuals who saw the situation from entirely different points of view. In August, 1833, Austin drew up a brief statement concerning Texas which was to be used to support the application for separate statehood, and during his detention in Mexico City he supplemented this with a more detailed explanation

[13]

of affairs, which was published in January, 1835. During the interval between these two statements the acting president dispatched Juan N. Almonte to Texas for the double purpose of making an accurate inspection of the province with a view to planning a military invasion if necessary and of delaying the supposedly impending outbreak and gaining time by promising reforms. Almonte spent from May until August, 1834, visiting the Anglo-American settlements; and following his return to Mexico he submitted to the government a detailed report on the population, resources, and activities in the province. This account was published in February, 1835, shortly after the appearance of Austin's second statement; and although the work of each man contains numerous statements which are contradictory to those of the other, each serves in general to supplement and confirm the other.

Austin estimated the total population of Texas at 46,500 in his statement of 1833, while Almonte placed it at 21,000 in 1834. There is no official information by which to check these estimates, but the most careful estimates by recent students have placed it at about 30,000, of whom probably one tenth were Mexicans. This population was scattered over the region between the Gulf Coast and the San Antonio–

Nacogdoches road, extending from the Sabine River to San Antonio—an area of about 50,000 square miles—but not all the land included within these limits was occupied by settlers in 1834. The two principal areas of Anglo-American settlement were around Nacogdoches, near the eastern border of the province, and along the Brazos and Colorado rivers, with San Felipe as the center. Practically all of the Mexican population was to be found in the region stretching southeastward from San Antonio to the coast, where it was separated from the Anglo-Americans by an unoccupied area varying from about twenty-five to seventy-five miles in width.

To govern this expanse of territory the first legislature of Coahuila-Texas had provided for the adoption of the Spanish system of local government, which meant that each community of more than one thousand inhabitants was to be organized into a municipality with the control of local matters in the hands of an *ayuntamiento,* or town council, to be elected by the people. These municipalities were to be grouped together into a department, administered by a political chief who was appointed by the governor and who was responsible for maintaining good order. All laws and instructions from the superior authorities, both state and national, had to be promulgated by him, and

[15]

he was the medium through which the citizens or the local agencies were supposed to communicate with those authorities.

In 1828 the state government created seven municipalities in Texas and placed them under the jurisdiction of the department of Bexar, whose political chief was to reside at San Antonio. At the beginning of 1834 there were still only seven municipalities, despite the fact that the population was at least three times as great as it had been at the time of their creation. The only suggestion of an effort to keep pace with the growing requirements of this rapidly increasing population had been the establishment in 1831 of the department of Nacogdoches, embracing the region north and east of Galveston Bay. Since this left the entire area lying west and south of that department under the jurisdiction of the political chief at San Antonio, whose interests were Mexican, it is somewhat easier to understand the concern felt by the Anglo-American inhabitants of the department of Bexar, who outnumbered the Mexicans by at least three to one. To them it seemed obvious that the machinery of local government needed to be adjusted to the changed conditions.

Even more serious than these shortcomings, however, was the lack of any set of courts for administering justice in Texas. The state constitution provided vaguely for a judicial system, but aside from the assumption of certain minor jurisdiction by local political officials and the establishment at Saltillo of a supreme court with appellate jurisdiction, nothing had been done to organize this branch of the government. Thus the settlers, far removed from the nearest organized court, were forced to fall back upon their own initiative and resourcefulness in their efforts to preserve order or to settle questions of property rights. When Almonte disparagingly described the custom of giving violators of laws a coat of tar and feathers and escorting them out of the community with a warning not to return, he failed to understand that this was merely the settlers' method of administering speedy punishment as a substitute for the inconveniences and delays involved in carrying a trial through the state courts, whose headquarters were several hundred miles away. The reminiscences of men and women who lived through these years in Texas contain numerous accounts of such summary administration of justice to counterfeiters, thieves, murderers, and other classes of offenders; and the method usually proved effective, for the culprit knew his judges too well to risk being caught a second time in the same community.

But this situation was shortly to be improved. About the same time that the requests concerning local government which Austin had taken to Mexico City were referred to the state government, a similar petition from the Mexican population at San Antonio reached the governor through the proper chain of officials. The two groups complained of the same problems, but the essential difference between their statements lay in the fact that the Mexican in Texas was calling upon a paternal government to come and help him, while the Anglo-American was begging to be allowed to help himself. Reassured to some extent by the refusal of the national authorities to grant separate statehood to Texas, the state legislature which met in 1834 sought to forestall further Anglo-American activity by making concessions in accordance with the spirit of the Mexican petition. The first step was the division of the department of Bexar in such manner that virtually the entire Mexican population remained under the jurisdiction of the political chief at San Antonio, while all of the Anglo-American section was incorporated in the new department of Brazos, with San Felipe as its capital. Other acts provided for the establishment of six new municipalities, for the use of English as well as Spanish in official and business transactions, and for the increase of the Texan representation in the state legislature to three members. Then, to meet the complaint concerning lack of judicial organization, the legislature passed an act providing for the division of Texas into three judicial districts with a district judge in each, while the entire region was placed under the jurisdiction of "the Superior Judicial Court of Texas," which was to hold sessions three times a year at each of the three departmental capitals. Provision was also made for the adoption of certain English common-law procedures and for trial by jury in both civil and criminal cases, with the interesting innovation that the agreement of eight jurymen out of twelve was sufficient for a verdict.

While the much-desired goal of separate statehood had not been attained, and although the state's orgy of political reorganization for Texas had not completely and satisfactorily removed all the vulnerable spots in its governmental machinery, it was obvious that the political status of the Anglo-American element had been considerably improved. Consequently many of the more conservative colonists were willing to accept the situation, even though it did not conform exactly to their idea of a thoroughly satisfactory arrangement. Austin himself was able to send word from his detached position in Mexico City that everything was now changed and that continued union with Coahuila was the object to be sought. In this way, he said, the Texans could continue to use constitutional means for gradually securing further reforms. Thus if the political situation had been the only problem with which these people were concerned, there would have been little cause for continued hostility to Mexican policies. But to the Texan the nature of his economic development and certain attendant social conditions also demanded attention, and toward these his interest was already turned.

Economically, the Anglo-American in Texas was advancing rapidly by 1834, and his increasing prosperity was due in large measure to his ability to take advantage of the agricultural possibilities of the country itself. Six years earlier Austin had said, with a sincerity of enthusiasm which would be an asset for the modern real-estate salesman: "Nature seems to have formed Texas for a great agricultural, grazing, manufacturing, and commercial country. . . . It combines in an eminent degree all the elements necessary for those different branches of industry." In 1833, however, he reported to the Mexican government that it was exclusively agricultural, the other "branches of industry" apparently remaining little more than potentialities. As a matter of fact his own early descriptions of the country, together with the character of the Mexican land policy, appealed primarily to the farmer rather than to the trader or manufacturer. Thus far the Anglo-Americans had been sufficiently resourceful to produce their own foodstuffs and at the same time to establish a reputation for producing the best quality of cotton that went to the New Orleans market. But they had also combined their agriculture with stock raising, and Almonte in 1834 estimated the number of livestock at about 75,000 head of cattle, something over 100,000 head of hogs, and nearly 10,000 head of sheep, practically all of them being found in the two departments occupied by the Anglo-Americans.

As a natural accompaniment to their successful agricultural and stock-raising enterprise, these people were becoming more and more conscious of the necessity for commercial expansion beyond the limits of their own province. The available information concerning their foreign commerce about 1834, while perhaps not always accurate as to totals, shows that the balance of trade was against them. They were exporting agricultural products and other raw materials amounting to about $500,000 annually, while their imports, consisting largely of manufactured articles such as clothing, shoes, implements, weapons, and other necessities, ran as high as $630,000 a year. It is not surprising, therefore, to find Almonte reporting that "money is very scarce in Texas, and one may say with certainty that out of every hundred transactions made not ten involve specie." The conviction was fast growing that without adequate market facilities for their surplus products economic progress would soon reach its limit; consequently no possibility was being overlooked. As articles of export they could offer cotton, corn, lumber, salted meats, hides, and even livestock, while the abundance of such wild animals as beavers, otters, bears, deer, and buffalo furnished an opportunity for the development of an important fur trade.

But the only market to which they had ready access was New Orleans, and since all these commodities were already available in the United States, they were forced to trade under unfavorable conditions. They were convinced that their produce could be sold at Vera Cruz or Matamoros for a higher price than at New Orleans, but the lack of shipping connections and the accompanying lack of a constructive commercial policy on the part of either the state or the national government in Mexico made this impossible. Perhaps the best evidence of the nature of the adjustment needed appeared in the fact that Austin, interested in obtaining separate statehood for Texas, and Almonte, desirous of ensuring closer relations between the Anglo-Americans and the Mexicans, described the same general economic conditions and suggested similar plans for carrying out their commercial programs. To both men it was evident that the best interests of Texas lay in the development of its trade with Mexico.

Austin presented statistics which showed that such commodities as cotton, corn, and lard could be sold in the Mexican markets for at least four times as much as they brought in New Orleans; "and the same proportion holds true," he said, "with reference to all the products of Texas." Almonte's interpretation of this same set of facts was indicated in his statement that the Mexicans were then buying from New Orleans merchants the same type of agricultural products that the Texans disposed of, but were paying higher prices than the Texan would have to charge if his produce could be sent directly to the Mexican ports. By diverting the Texan exports to Mexico the margin of profits made by the United States interests would be eliminated and all parts of the Mexican republic would be benefited economically, while a more important consideration would be the growth of a more definite community of interests between the inhabitants of Texas and those of Mexico proper. His proposed solution was for the Mexican government to provide the necessary encouragement by adjusting its tariff system and by making definite appropriations for the development of coastwise trading facilities. Austin mentioned both plans as desirable and went a step farther by urging that Texas could adjust itself more easily to such a policy if it was relieved from its subservience to the Coahuilan majority, which lacked commercial interests.

Both men also argued that commerce by land from the ports of Texas to the interior states presented advantages almost equal in value to the coastwise trade. Pointing out that each year about two million dollars worth of merchandise entered New Mexico and Chihuahua from Missouri, Austin said: "This commerce is entirely outside the course which the geographical situation of the country and nature itself has marked out; the ports of Texas were evidently designed for it." The advantages which Mexico would derive from the encouragement of such trade would be the substitution of Mexican ports for those of the United States as starting points for the merchants, an increase in the receipts of the maritime customhouses, a distribution of merchandise to the people of the interior at lower cost, and the attraction

of settlers to the vast uninhabited districts of the
interior.

Such was the vision of the commercial possibilities
for Texas in 1834. The presence of such prospects
was proof that the province had reached a turning
point in its economic growth, and had the Mexican
authorities been in a position to give their undivided
and sympathetic attention to the accordant features
in the report of their own inspector and that of the
Texas agent, they could have removed almost at a
single stroke the chief basis for discontent. The Texans admitted that they needed Mexican markets, and
Almonte showed that trade with Texas would be an
economic benefit to Mexico. The solution seemed
obvious, and the Texans could not comprehend the
failure of the Mexican government to take favorable
action. They realized that their ability to outstrip
the Mexicans in economic development had been due
partly to the fact that their distance from the capital
gave them a favored position out of reach of the
civil wars which had devastated Mexican resources,
and they wanted to retain the possibility of devoting
themselves to industry and commerce without inter-
ruption. But instead of blaming domestic strife in
Mexico for the scant consideration of their petitions
and plans, many Texans followed their first impulse

and concluded that the official attitude was due to a reluctance to work out any policy which would reflect to the advantage of the non-Mexican inhabitants of the republic; and their resentment was not lessened as a result of this conclusion.

But the interest of the Texans during this period of transition was not absorbed entirely in political and economic problems. To most of them a desire for social adjustment was intimately connected with the efforts to secure more efficient administration and better commercial and industrial opportunities. Gradually the realization had dawned upon them that they were no longer the isolated frontiersmen of the previous decade. "Within four miles of me there are more than one thousand inhabitants, chiefly new emigrants," wrote an early settler in 1834, "and within the same distance we have four small stores, two blacksmith shops and two schools. We have a dancing frolick every week and preaching allmost every Sunday." This meant that increasing immigration had shattered their sense of insularity, and in place of the individual whose first instinct was to rely upon his own self-sufficiency there had been substituted the community, with mutual interests bringing about a stronger feeling of interdependence. In a measure this social transformation was due to the synchronous economic development; but it also had become increasingly significant as a contributing factor in determining the nature of further progress, both political and economic, and it was therefore one of the important elements of local conditions in Texas in 1834.

The growth of such community interests and the sense of interdependence naturally developed homogeneity in society, and it was already possible to detect mutual interests centering around the absence of certain desirable social institutions. Two such deficiencies—the absence of public religious worship and the lack of proper educational facilities—were beginning to attract attention by 1834, and the interest of the colonists in these questions was almost sure to become a factor in determining their attitude toward their government. For the average Anglo-American of the second quarter of the nineteenth century the church and the school were necessary adjuncts of a civilized community, but he had developed the theory that religion was not subject to state supervision while the encouragement of education was one of the functions of the state. The immigrant who came from the United States to Texas found in the Mexican attitude on these questions a direct contravention of his own theory. Technically, the Mexican citizen was required to accept the religion which the state specified but was left free to develop or to neglect his schools as he pleased. The alternatives open to the immigrant, therefore, were either to adjust himself to the Mexican conception or to convince the Mexican authorities that their conception was wrong. During the earlier years of the colonial period neither the religious nor the educational problem had presented any serious difficulties, but by 1834 changing conditions had gradually led to the possibility of misunderstanding in connection with both.

The religious requirements of the Mexican government had been clearly understood by the early settlers, and they had come with an apparent willingness to adjust themselves to the situation. To them the mere form of religious worship could not be permitted to interfere with such an excellent opportunity of bettering their economic condition; consequently they were ready to conform, at least outwardly. But when the Mexican authorities consistently neglected to check up on the religious affiliation of the newcomers, the settlers could scarcely be expected to take the initiative in adopting the Catholic faith. On the other hand, either they had no real enthusiasm for the Protestant worship or they felt that it would not be wise to stir the Mexican authorities from indifference by establishing their own churches. As a result religious life was reduced almost to the vanishing point during the first decade of Anglo-American colonization, and there is little evidence that the situation caused any worry among the settlers themselves. A priest appeared among them at irregular intervals—usually from one to two years apart—but instead of attempting to furnish spiritual guidance he merely performed such acts as were necessary to enable the colonists to comply with the legal requirements of a state religion. In general, therefore, burials were conducted without benefit of clergy; the children were given names without formal ceremony; and those who desired could get their spiritual inspiration by reading their Bibles at home.

But the fact that under Mexican law no marriage ceremony was recognized as legal unless it was performed by a Catholic priest presented a practical need for at least one form of religious services. To meet this problem the Texans worked out an arrangement, based on the idea of civil marriages, by which parties wishing to be married were allowed to go before a local official and sign a bond agreeing to submit to the ceremony of the church as soon as an opportunity was offered. The infrequent visits of the priest became the signal for large gatherings of friends and neighbors at the most commodious houses, where all classes of matrimonial candidates, including those previously married by non-Catholic agencies, those living together under bond, and young men and maidens, would be gathered as many as possible into one room to have the ceremony performed for the entire group at once. On such occasions, also, a number of people usually presented themselves for baptism in order to meet the letter of the regulation that only Catholics could own land. But in either case these people were formally complying with the religious ceremonies as a mere legal requirement, and the cases were rare in which they were willing to forfeit their claims to property or the legitimacy of their children on account of religious scruples. Under these circumstances it would have been difficult for the Texans to contend that their obligations to the established church constituted a burden. If there was any just ground for complaint, it was not that they were oppressed in religious matters, but that even their practical ecclesiastical needs were taken care of too infrequently.

After 1830, however, such a status became increasingly difficult to maintain. New immigrants continued to arrive in spite of the law of April 6, 1830, and a large proportion of the newcomers became

squatters on unoccupied land or purchased small hold-
ings from those settlers who were willing to subdivide
their property. Having had no dealings directly with
the Mexican authorities, they were not impressed
with the desirability of complying with various regulations—in fact their presence was itself a violation
of one specific regulation—and many of them did not
attempt to adjust themselves or to analyze the existing situation and appraise their own position in it. A
complicating element appeared in the fact that just
at this time the people of the western part of the
United States were experiencing an intense religious
enthusiasm which manifested itself in revival meetings. Coming, as many of these settlers did, while
the influence of this religious fervor was still strong
within them, one of the first things to impress them
was the absence of churches, and their shocked senses
called a missionary zeal to the surface. It was only
natural, therefore, that during this period the camp-
meeting movement penetrated into Texas; and by the
end of 1834 churches had been organized throughout
the northeastern part of the province by the Baptists,
Methodists, and Cumberland Presbyterians, while
settlers in other sections were beginning to feel that
toleration would soon become the definite policy of
the government. In the meantime the state legislature

had adopted what seemed to be a spirit of concession on the religious question by tacking to a new land law a provision that "no person shall be molested on account of his political or religious opinions, provided he does not disturb public order." Whether this meant complete freedom in the organization of Protestant churches in Texas cannot be determined, for the authorities soon found themselves too busy with other problems to give any serious thought to the religious situation.

But while the Texans were making these inroads into the established relation between church and state in Mexico, they were proving less successful in their efforts to obtain concessions to their interpretation of the state's responsibility for providing educational opportunity. Strictly speaking, the real difference between the Anglo-American and the Mexican attitude on public education lay not so much in theory as in application. The constitution of Coahuila-Texas specified that the methods of instruction should be uniform throughout the state and required the legislature to formulate a general plan for a system of public schools. Numerous laws had been passed to implement this requirement, but none of them had been effectively enforced; and both Austin and Almonte reported that there were no schools or academies in

Texas endowed or maintained by the state. The convention of 1832 had formulated a petition for a grant of land for the promotion of education, but no action was taken on this request. Consequently the people of Texas were forced to continue the development of their schools through private initiative, and such scattered and fragmentary information as has been found indicates that at least twenty private schools had been established since the beginning of Anglo-American colonization and that no less than ten of these were in operation at some time during the period 1833–35.

As if these fundamental questions of securing satisfactory arrangements in their general political, economic, and social conditions were not enough to keep the Texans fully occupied, certain special difficulties were gradually demanding more and more attention. For example, the facilities for adequate communication between the different parts of the province had not kept pace with increasing needs, and the Anglo-Americans were trying with little success to interest the state government in the development of a program of internal improvements which would provide good roads and improve the usability of the numerous streams. They were also concerned over the ever present danger of depredations from the Indian tribes along their frontier, but the only response that came to their requests for permission to organize their own militia force was a suggestion from the government that convict troops would be sent to handle the problem. More serious than either of these, however, was the adoption by the state legislature of 1834 of a new series of land laws by which the *empresario* system was abolished and the gates apparently opened to speculation on a wholesale plan. To the Texans this seemed to mean the concentration of land in the hands of a few at the expense of the people in general, and from their point of view the whole episode furnished a clearer illustration of the defectiveness of the state government.

So many questions of vital importance had been raised within this short period and so few had been settled, that it was becoming increasingly evident that from several points of view Texas had reached a turning point in its development. The importance of the period lay in the fact that it marked the cumulation of hitherto diversified frontier interests into one general problem of securing a satisfactory adjustment to the changing conditions which accentuated the difference between the Texans and the rest of the Mexican republic. While it was true that a certain sense of incompatibility had been present from the beginning of Anglo-American colonization, it was equally true that the pacifying influence of Stephen F. Austin had thus far made compromise a possibility. But through the fatuity of the Mexican government Austin was being detained in Mexico City while Texas was awakening to its real needs, with the result that both sides were deprived of the services of the one man who might have found an equitable solution for the problem. Certainly Texas had not yet developed a substitute who possessed his understanding of the situation and his power of inspiring men with confidence in his leadership; and it was during this period of leaderless and futile attempts at realization of economic possibilities, at stabilization of social developments, at adjustments in political organization, and at the solution of other problems of special significance that the seeds were sown which were eventually to germinate into an open revolt against the uncertainties and inefficiencies of Mexican rule.

II

THE PRELIMINARIES TO THE
REVOLUTION

A RAPID survey of the situation in Texas about the end of 1834 serves to emphasize the fact that the various problems for which the Anglo-Americans were trying to obtain a solution during their period of transition did not in themselves seem to furnish sufficient cause for a revolt against Mexican rule. One of the strongest arguments against hostility was to be found in the concessions already being made to them by the authorities of the joint state. The new land legislation alone might have caused trouble, but when the same session of the legislature took up the petitions which had been referred to it by Santa Anna's officials, the only reasonable course was to await developments. Although a radical faction had gradually taken form beginning with the disturbances of 1832, its principal accomplishment thus far had been the petition for separate statehood, but that it did not look upon this as an ultimatum was shown by the fact that the news of the adverse action of the Mexican authorities found it without a program for further procedure. And when, during 1834, measures were enacted providing for the establishment of new municipalities, the creation of the new department of Brazos, and the organization of the judicial system for Texas, and granting various other requests which had been included in the petitions, the position of the conservative element was strengthened. Even the desired assistance in the development of schools and the adoption of a constructive policy with regard to coastwise trade might be expected to come as soon as the national authorities could give proper attention to them. Perhaps the most serious cause for concern in the whole picture at this time was the fact that Austin was still a prisoner in Mexico City.

The real power of Austin's influence in Texas was indicated in the fact that even after definite information concerning his arrest and the apparent failure of his mission had reached the Texans, they were willing to follow his advice that they remain tranquil and continue to adhere to Mexico and the Mexican confederation. His first thought after his arrest was to prevent turbulence when the news should reach Texas, and in the letters which he hastened to write to friends he constantly urged loyalty on the ground that any other attitude might prove harmful to Texas. Consequently, although there was much excitement when the news arrived, his advice was taken so literally that the people did not even dare to formulate a petition to the authorities in his behalf until he had sent a specific request that this be done. While this hesitation was undoubtedly due largely to a fear that any move might militate against him, it indicated also that without a leader to suggest the procedure the people were at a loss for a plan of action. Since his was the only leadership they had known, they now seemed to prefer even his long-distance counsel to that of other men who had previously played secondary roles. As a temporary situation this might not have proved serious, for during the first year of his absence the nearest approach to unified action among the Texans usually came in connection with attempts to carry out what they thought would be Austin's policy. But as his detention was prolonged through 1834 and into the following year, his grasp upon affairs in Texas was naturally weakened, and the way was opened for the development of factional groups under the influence of men who lacked his power of commanding the respect and confidence of the whole population.

During his absence some of these groups began to merge into a so-called war party under the nominal leadership of William H. Wharton, who was outspoken in his opposition to Austin's policy of compromise and conciliation. Within a short time Wharton's following included most of the disgruntled spirits who had at some time disagreed with Austin. In general, however, the common ground of members of this group was not personal animosity toward Austin himself but merely the fact that they honestly differed with him on the question of the best means of advancing the interests of Texas. None of them could justly be charged with a lack of sincerity, and perhaps had any of them carried Austin's responsibilities they would have equaled him in caution. Without such a burden they were free to criticize without being constructive, while he was forced to count the possible cost for his colonists at every important turn. But they demonstrated their unwillingness to be precipitated into hostilities when Anthony Butler, the United States chargé d'affaires in Mexico, sought to take advantage of Austin's absence by sending into Texas anonymous letters in which he asserted that Santa Anna had threatened to convert the region into a desert. This was followed by a warning that only their own energy could save them from the fate that

Mexico had planned, and the example of revolution-ary Yucatan was cited, with the insinuating statement that "surely what they have done you can do." Clearly the purpose of these letters was to incite the Texans to an overt act of rebellion from which they could not retreat, but he reckoned without knowledge of the general sentiment in Texas. Despite his attempts at anonymity the letters were recognized and condemned as his handiwork; and even though they came into the hands of Austin's opponents, no effort was made to use them, and the people remained quiet. It was evi-dent that no one in Texas was sufficiently excited to begin a rebellion on the basis of rumor or propaganda.

It was also during Austin's absence that confusion concerning the new land laws of the state government spread over Texas and that some of his closest asso-ciates, unable to turn to him for advice, added to the complexity of the situation by becoming involved in the speculation which followed. As the average Texan watched a few individuals obtain grants of land run-ning into several million acres, his attention was fixed on what seemed to him an improvident and perhaps even a malevolent waste of the public lands at the expense of the people of the province, so that he failed to see that these laws were in reality a part of the state's effort to protect itself against a new threat of interference in its affairs by the national authorities in Mexico City. During the intermittent periods when Santa Anna had left the administration of public affairs in the hands of an acting president, the liberal element in Mexico had attempted numerous reforms which threatened the privileges of both the army and the clergy, and the stage was set for a reactionary movement fostered by those influential interests. They drew up the so-called plan of Cuernavaca in May, 1834, in which they denounced all liberal reforms and called upon the president to uphold the constitutional safeguards by dissolving the congress and ruling as dictator. Acceding to this demand, Santa Anna dismissed the congress and proceeded to rule the country not only without a congress but also without a council of government, and even without ministers; and at first without any opposition or obstacles. As his program was extended to the disbanding of state legislatures and the deposing of governors, serious discontent developed in the northern and eastern states, while in Coahuila the opposition became involved in a purely local controversy over the location of the state capital.

This local conflict had been started in 1833 by an act of the legislature providing for the removal of the capital from Saltillo, in the southeastern corner of Coahuila, to Monclova, nearer the center of the province. After refusing to participate in the legislative sessions at Monclova, the Saltillo adherents set up a rival governor and issued a pronouncement declaring all laws passed at the new capital to be null and void. In the confusion which followed, it became impossible to hold the regular election of state officials in 1834, and the contention was raised that Coahuila-Texas was now entirely without a lawful political organization. At this point the Texans became concerned about the developments. The threat of the Saltillo faction to invalidate the work of the Monclova session of the legislature brought up a possibility that their interests might become involved in the outcome of the controversy, for all of the recent legislative acts affecting conditions in Texas had been passed during that session. Consequently an effort was made by members of the war party to take advantage of the confusion by calling for a convention to meet at San Antonio, either to organize a provisional government or to decide what other steps should be taken. But the conservatives, still seeking to follow Austin's earlier counsel, issued a warning against reckless measures and pointed out that since the federal constitution of 1824 was still in force, a separate state government could lawfully be established under it.

They also sought to show that the existing Mexican government and President Santa Anna entertained the most friendly feelings toward Texas; that any attempt to effect forcibly a separation from Coahuila would invite fresh difficulties and prolong Austin's imprisonment or perhaps even endanger his life; that Texas was prosperous, thanks to excellent crops and a large immigration; and, in short, that if the people would be patient their grievances would be remedied in the end. As a result, the proposal for holding a convention was rejected. Thus for the second time within a year the Texans had demonstrated their determination to avoid being plunged into a conflict with the Mexican authorities.

Meanwhile Santa Anna ordered that an election be held for the purpose of choosing legitimate state officials, and about the same time federal troops were sent to Coahuila, ostensibly for the purpose of restoring order. Following the election General Martin Perfecto de Cos, brother-in-law of Santa Anna and commander of the troops, attempted to interfere with the work of the new legislature, and it retaliated by authorizing the governor to collect the militia for the defense of the state government and to pay for this service by a loan based on the state's revenues. On finding an empty treasury the governor turned to the possibilities offered in the new land laws and began at once the sale of land on a large scale in order to obtain the necessary money, and it was this action that aroused the suspicion of the Texans just enough to bring about a misunderstanding of the actual situation.

The real danger lay in the fact that Santa Anna was rapidly maturing his plans for the centralization of the national authority in his own hands. A new congress had been convened to preserve the appearance of federalism, but its members showed their subservience by passing such laws as the president demanded. After expressly annulling the Coahuilan land laws and reducing the state militias to one man for every five hundred inhabitants, this congress indicated its future course by declaring that it possessed the power to make such changes in the constitution as it thought to be for the benefit of the nation, without subjecting itself to the obstacles and delays that the constitution prescribed. By the end of March, 1835, only the states of Zacatecas and Coahuila remained recalcitrant; and in April, Santa Anna put himself at the head of an army to compel the former to accept the plan of Cuernavaca. In the meantime General Cos had been sent to watch the situation in Coahuila, and his interference with the legislature was primarily to find a pretext for moving troops to the state to prevent the development of an open insurrection. Thus the issue, which was now clearly drawn, turned upon the preservation or destruction of the federal form of government established by the constitution of 1824. But when the governor appealed to the Texans for assistance against Cos, his call was looked upon as a design to promote the interests of the speculators, and they refused to respond. From their point of view the overthrow of the state authorities would benefit Texas; consequently they remained indifferent to the struggle in Coahuila while Cos steadily advanced and the governor and legislature sought refuge in Texas to escape capture. As one writer has aptly explained their attitude: "The speculators were a stench in the nostrils of the average citizen, and to his mind all the alarmists were tarred with the same stick. His conviction that their solicitude for the public weal was calculated to advance their own interests blinded him for a time to the real significance of what was going on in Mexico City."

It was not long, however, before the Texans were disillusioned by developments nearer home. As Santa Anna's program of centralization advanced, it was inevitable that his attention should be turned to Texas as a part of the obstinate state of Coahuila, and he found an excuse in reports that a contraband trade was being carried on by way of Texan ports to avoid the payment of tariff duties at Matamoros. Cos was told, therefore, to provide for the reopening of the customhouses on an effective basis, which he undertook to do by appointing Colonel Domingo de Ugartechea to serve as military commander of Texas, with headquarters at San Antonio. When Ugartechea established a collector of customs at Velasco and deputy collectors at two other points early in 1835, the stage was set for a repetition of the events of 1832. After several weeks of semipassive resistance, the merchants finally formulated a protest against the discriminations shown at various ports, and in June one of their leaders was arrested and thrown into prison at Anahuac. News of this affair reached San Felipe about the same time as the reports from Coahuila concerning the overthrow of the state government, and the first reaction was a suspicion that there might be collusion between the speculators and the merchants to precipitate an outbreak which would benefit both groups but which would not help Texas as a whole. This spirit tempered the information which was carried from San Felipe to the other communities, with the result that meetings were called in various parts of the province to protest against the tendency toward refusal to submit to the enforcement of the laws.

Before action could be taken, however, new developments increased the uncertainty. On June 21 the people of San Felipe intercepted an official messenger from General Cos and on searching him found letters to the commander at Anahuac containing definite indications of the plans of the central government. One from Cos acknowledged the receipt of complaints about the attitude of the merchants and stated that the government could be expected to attend to the matter with the promptness which its importance demanded. Cos explained, also, that a battalion of troops had been ordered to Texas, to be distributed throughout the province as needed. Another letter, written by Ugartechea, said that "in a very short time the affairs of Texas will be definitely settled, for which purpose the government has ordered to take the line of march a strong division composed of the troops which were in Zacatecas, and which are now in Saltillo."

This information threw the Texans into a quandary. Their real desire was to avoid a break with the Mexican authorities, and they had hoped to accomplish this by preserving an attitude of strict neutrality. They knew, however, that they doubted the motives of the speculators, that they questioned the desirability of the demonstrations of the merchants, and that they objected to the extension of military authority. They saw also that if they opposed the speculators and merchants they should welcome the troops as an aid in checking undesirable activities, but this position was untenable if the coming of the troops meant the establishment of garrisons in Texas. On the other hand, if they opposed the threatened advance of the troops, they found themselves collaborating with the speculators. Their problem was increased by the lack of adequate information, combined with the slowness of communication and the consequent difficulty of obtaining concerted and simultaneous action throughout the province. They felt that time was needed in which to reach an understanding upon the most desirable plan of procedure, and consequently they sought to prevent the precipitation of a crisis by delaying action on issues which they did not comprehend; but such a position soon became difficult to maintain.

The disclosures of June 21 at San Felipe seemed to place the advantage temporarily on the side of the war party. Under the influence of the excitement which followed, the political chief issued a proclamation calling upon the men of the department of Brazos to "turn out immediately, organize," and march to the assistance of the governor, and suggestions were made that San Antonio should be occupied at once in order to prevent it from being used by Cos as a base of operations against Texas. Resolutions condemning Santa Anna's "total disregard for the rights of the states" were approved, and the people pledged themselves to maintain the governor and all state officials in the discharge of their duties and to uphold the federal and state constitutions as originally adopted. The more radical element apparently held a secret meeting, presided over by the political chief, in which William B. Travis was authorized to organize an expedition against the Mexicans at Anahuac. A week later he attacked the post and received the surrender of its entire garrison.

But such indications of a warlike sentiment emanating from San Felipe were not allowed to go unchallenged by the other communities of Texas. Up to this point a majority of the people had assumed the attitude of indifferent spectators, apparently determined to take no part in the discussions of either the war or the peace advocates. Now, however, unless they were willing to accept the aggressive program implied in the attack on Anahuac, they were forced to drop their aloofness. Aggression might lead to an open break, and since their inclinations were against action, they were drawn naturally toward the side of opposition to the war spirit. The neighboring municipality of Columbia adopted a protest "against the acts and conduct of any set of individuals (less than a majority) calculated to involve the citizens of Texas in a conflict with the Federal Government of Mexico" and recommended "union, moderation, organization, and strict adherence to the laws and constitution of the land." By the time Travis had returned from Anahuac, a number of communities had approved the Columbia resolutions or had passed others of a similar nature; and as this conciliatory disposition gained force he found himself the target for criticism from almost every meeting that was held. Even his own community of San Felipe invited the captured commander of Anahuac to attend a meeting to see for himself that "it was not by the vote of the majority nor by the will of the inhabitants that those persons were authorized to commit that outrage against the supreme government."

By the end of July, Travis himself was convinced that the majority favored peace, and he suggested to a friend that the war party had "better be quiet and settle down for awhile." He wrote to Ugartechea that "there only wants a good understanding between the Government and the people of Texas to set all things right," and expressed his willingness to assist in bring-

ing about such an understanding. He also asked the
people to suspend judgment on his act until he could
make an explanation. But Travis was not the only one
who was convinced by the developments during July
that the sincerity and strength of the conservative
group provided an effective check upon the agitations
of the war party. The political chief soon began to
feel that part of the criticism being directed against
belligerent activities applied also to his hasty action
in issuing the call for volunteers and his participation
in the secret meeting at San Felipe; therefore, he now
hastened to declare himself in cordial agreement with
the spirit of the Columbia resolutions. In an attempt
to apologize for his earlier action, he suggested "that
we always act with caution." "The late unnecessary
alarm," he said, "proceeding out of false information,
has taught this salutary lesson of caution and moderation." Then, finding that this gesture did not allay
the criticism, he relinquished his office after naming a
member of the peace party to serve in his place. About
the same time, one of Ugartechea's agents reported
that the great majority of the people of Texas were
peaceable, law-abiding Mexican citizens who would
support any conciliatory measures; and from the side
of the conservatives one of the most ardent advocates
of peace wrote from San Felipe that "all here is in a

train for peace, the war and speculating parties are entirely put down, and are preparing to leave the country."

During the entire month of July and the first two weeks of August popular meetings were held in most of the Anglo-American communities in Texas. With three exceptions every meeting for which the proceedings are available expressed suspicion that the dangers were being exaggerated by special interests and pledged itself to "sustain the legal authorities in the exercise of their constitutional duties." The persistent recurrence of such expressions of loyalty to Mexico might have been taken as an indication of sincerity had they not been inspired by a feeling that recent events made explanation necessary in order to maintain peace. The Texans themselves realized that under ordinary conditions the sentiment which was now being expressed so carefully would have been taken for granted, and they also realized that they needed more complete information to assist them in reaching a decision concerning their ultimate position. Consequently a second common idea running through the resolutions of these meetings was the need for "some medium through which public opinion can be ascertained and wielded with effect against the irregularities of those whose indifference to the laws of the country has destroyed the mutual confidence."

Several communities acted upon this idea by appointing delegates to form a joint committee, which was authorized to adopt such measures as seemed "best calculated to promote the welfare of Texas." On July 15 this committee began its work by preparing an address to the inhabitants of the department of Brazos, in which it stated that there was no just cause for immediate alarm and expressed "the most sanguine hopes that the present commotion will be quieted and good order restored without any collision with the Federal Troops." It declined to issue a call for a general convention, on the ground that such a move would probably be regarded by the authorities as preliminary to a rebellion, and it appointed two commissioners to visit Cos at Matamoros to explain the recent occurrences and to assure him of the fidelity of the people to the government.

Although the general situation seemed to indicate that the ascendancy of the peace party was secure, the controlling factor in this appearance of security was the realization on the part of the Texans that they lacked adequate information about the actual state of affairs. The joint committee had found it impossible to issue an explanation of the situation because it was unable to reconcile the many conflicting reports which it received concerning the developments in Mexico and the attitude of the authorities toward the Texans. A significant feature of each protestation of loyalty had been the repeated emphasis on their willingness to obey any requirements that might be placed upon them by constitutional methods, and this implied opposition to any attempt to ignore or violate the constitution. If some of the current rumors proved to be true, such a stand would be equivalent to a rebellion against the plans of President Santa Anna; but for the Texans this issue had not yet been clearly drawn. Thus it was felt that until it could be proved conclusively that the rights and the interests of the people were in jeopardy, it would be unwise to make any new move which might provoke the Mexicans to action, and therefore even the militant members of the committee accepted a program of watchful waiting.

With the developments among the Texans thus tending definitely toward peace, any change of direction would obviously depend upon the reaction of the Mexican officials to the events which had already taken place. Hence a little tact on the part of Cos and Ugartechea at this time would have increased the probability of continued peace, but they could hardly be expected to have known this. They were already suspicious of the Texans; consequently the Anahuac affair seemed to them simply an expression of the popular will, showing, as Ugartechea said, "the disaffection and discontent with which those wicked ones look at the Nation." But their first move indicated a desire to avoid conflict. On July 7, Ugartechea wrote to the political chief of the department of Brazos a letter, which he no doubt expected to be made public, assuring him that the troops which had been ordered to Texas were merely to garrison the ports and to protect the country from the Indians. He had already suggested that Cos issue a proclamation to that effect, and on July 12, Cos followed this advice by writing to the three political chiefs in Texas a long circular letter in which he attempted to show that the lack of a proper police force in the province had "necessarily contributed to the introduction of many men without country, morality, or any employment" and that these men were trying to foment a revolution by arguing that the supreme government was opposed to the interests of the Texans. He then explained that the coming of the troops was not intended to mean the beginning of military subjection but was to give the people "a guard more in favor of than against their security," and he concluded by assuring "the honest residents" that "so long as they remain attached to the Government and the Laws they have nothing to fear," and requesting that "whatever pretensions the inhabitants may have they will please manifest them by legal means to the Government."

But while Cos and Ugartechea were thus assuring the Texans of the beneficent intentions of the government, they were also becoming involved in plans destined to destroy any conciliatory effect that their assurances might have had. Despite the fact that one of his agents had persistently warned him that if he wanted to avoid a break he should refrain from sending troops into the department of Brazos, Ugartechea determined to make an example of the leaders in the attack on Anahuac. On July 13, therefore, he asked Cos for mounted troops to enable him "to punish acts so scandalous and to repulse force by force." A few days later, having learned of the resentment being expressed in Texas against some of the leaders of the war party and the speculators, he issued an order for the arrest of Travis and five other men, who, he said, "are actually conspiring against the government," and after receiving the approval of Cos for this action he announced that if they were not surrendered he would proceed at the head of his cavalry to execute the order.

As was to be expected, this move served to antagonize the Anglo-Americans and to destroy the advantage which had been gained by the peace party. Reports of the impending use of military force to effect the arrests spread rapidly, and the appearance at the same time of a Mexican schooner of war at Anahuac became the occasion for rumors that the coast was being blockaded and that troops were being landed to strengthen Ugartechea's force. These rumors provided the signal for a renewal of the activities of the war party, and it soon became evident that even the peace party was opposed to the military occupation of Texas, while most of its members were unwilling to surrender the citizens demanded by Cos and Ugartechea. The first sign of this turn in the tide of public opinion appeared in the tacit approval of peace and war party alike when the political chief temporized long enough for the intended victims to get out of reach before he issued the necessary orders for their arrest. In fact, two of them were sent on a mission to the department of Nacogdoches for the purpose of enlarging the field of activities. There they found that most of the people seemed to oppose action, and they succeeded in obtaining nothing more than a promise of assistance if any part of Texas should be attacked by an armed force.

In the meantime the developments in the department of Brazos began to converge more rapidly toward united action. On August 8, David G. Burnet, one of the leaders of the peace party, drew up a resolution in which he declared that "the turbulence of a distracted republic [would be] incomparably preferable to that sickly quietude of a military despotism." Pointing out that it was "impracticable for a people so dispersed as are the people of Texas to act collectively and in unison in any public exigency requiring deliberation and interchange of opinions," he urged that a general convention be called "to confer on the state of public affairs; to devise and carry into execution such measures as may be necessary to preserve good order and the due administration of the laws; to collect and distribute information relative to the nature and the operation of the new government of Mexico; to communicate with the authorities of that government; and to adopt and to carry into execution such ultimate measures as in their wisdom may seem meet and proper and conducive to the substantial, permanent welfare of Texas." This succinct statement of the need for a convention was an effective expression of the one point on which most of the Texans were in agreement, and by the middle of August each municipality had pledged itself to work toward that end. But since the joint committee had adjourned without calling such a conference, there was no longer an agency through which it might be called. The real need was for a self-constituted leader, and this was supplied when William H. Wharton, who was generally recognized as the head of the war party, induced the municipality of Columbia to appoint a committee of fifteen members to take the initial step.

This committee immediately began its work by appointing confidential agents to secure the co-operation of the other communities and by planning for the collection of funds to pay such expenses as might be incurred. On August 20 it issued an address in which it explained that since "centralism with the rapidity of magic has succeeded our late confederated form of government . . . we occupy the unenviable attitude of a people who have not a shadow of a legitimate government." This confused state of affairs would lead to a loss of confidence both at home and abroad, would cause immigration to cease, would increase the danger of having the remainder of their lands trifled away by unscrupulous speculators, and might enable a few rash individuals to plunge them into war without their consent. "Some seem to imagine," the committee said, "that the present difficulties can be quieted by remaining inactive and venting their endless and unavailing curses on the heads of the land speculators, and war party, as they are termed." Because it felt that this confusion could be cleared up only by "a consultation of all Texas through her representatives," the committee proposed that each municipality elect five individuals to convene at Washington-on-the-Brazos on October 15, with instructions "to secure peace if it is to be obtained on constitutional terms, and to prepare for war, if war be inevitable." It believed that such a conference would be sure to represent the opinion of Texas and that its decision should be accepted as final, even if it required Texans "to yield in servile submission to a form of government or to anything else that would disgrace us as free born men."

This proposal received general endorsement throughout Texas, the only amendment being offered by the Nacogdoches committee of safety to the effect that the number of representatives from each municipality should be raised from five to seven. Travis wrote exultingly from San Felipe that while he had been disgusted at the developments of the past six weeks, "it is different now, thank God! Principle has triumphed over prejudice, passion, cowardice, and slavery. Texas is herself again. . . . A tremendous reaction has taken place and the tories are almost as bad off as they were in 1832."

It soon became evident, however, that he was prematurely optimistic. In its eagerness to ensure satisfactory action, the committee began the dissemination of information by publishing letters, from which the signatures were withheld, in which the general situation was discussed and arguments presented in favor of a consultation. Among these were accounts of Santa Anna's projected military occupation of Texas, and some of them were recognized as communications which had already been branded by the peace party as propaganda. Nearly two months had passed since their original appearance, and the threatened invasion had not materialized. Moreover, Ugartechea had not followed up his threat to use force in securing the arrests which he had demanded three weeks earlier. Lulled into a feeling of security by this apparent inactivity among the Mexican officials, many of the conservatives began to suspect that this new move might be simply a renewal of the plans of the speculators to promote their own interests. Hence, while they generally agreed that the consultation should be held, they began a contest within the municipalities to control the selection of delegates in order to guarantee a peaceful adjustment. The spirit of factionalism was rapidly returning when, on September 1, Stephen F. Austin arrived in Texas from his long imprisonment in Mexico, and all elements immediately turned to him for a solution of the problem.

Before leaving Mexico City, Austin had advised the authorities that "no troops should be sent to Texas, and no cruisers along the coast," and while on the way home he had written to his cousin in Kentucky that he knew nothing about the state of public opinion in Texas. He assumed, however, that the people meant "to avoid all collision with Mexico if possible to do so, and be also ready to repel attacks should they come." His observations and reflections during his detention had convinced him that the federal system of 1824 was being destroyed and that Santa Anna could not be trusted. As a result, he was gradually coming to the conclusion that the ultimate solution to the problem must be complete separation from Mexico, but that this end should be attained slowly and quietly to avoid offending Mexican national dignity. "The more the American population of Texas is increased," he said, "the more readily will the Mexican government give it up; also, the more the people of Texas *seem* to oppose a separation from Mexico, the less tenacious will they be to hold it."

But his hope of finding the province "at peace and in tranquility" was shattered when the ship on which he had sailed from New Orleans to Texas encountered a Mexican schooner off the mouth of the Brazos River and succeeded in landing its passengers only after a battle. The impression made by this incident was strengthened when he began to receive requests for advice from individuals and committees in all parts of Texas. Therefore, with full knowledge that the people were waiting for an expression of his opinion, he accepted an invitation to speak at a public dinner at Brazoria on September 8. After a careful analysis of the situation, he concluded that since the rights and property of the Texans were in jeopardy, his desire for peaceful aggression was no longer feasible; and in a prepared address he announced his unequivocal support of the call for a consultation, which should "decide what representations ought to be made to the general government, and what ought to be done in future."

As a result of this announcement the last semblance of opposition to the consultation quickly disappeared. On September 12 the citizens of San Felipe, where this opposition had been strongest, adopted resolutions approving the call and appointed a committee to co-operate with other communities in securing united action. Because of Austin's acknowledged leadership in this committee, common consent seemed to accord to it the entire direction of affairs, and with his characteristic energy he began to formulate plans for securing a full representation. In a circular letter of September 13 he explained that instead of trying to organize a local government under the constitution of 1824 the consultation should deliberate on the question of calling a plenary convention for this purpose; and in order that "the necessary rules and regulations for directing elections and apportioning the representation equally, according to the population, the place where, and the time when the Convention ought to meet" might be settled, the delegates should come with definite instructions, and should bring with them "an exact census of the population, and return of the militia from their districts, to lay before the General Consultation." This proposal was accepted by the other communities, but since some of the committees questioned the propriety of a suggestion that the meeting place of the consultation be changed from Washington to San Felipe in order that a printing press might be accessible, Travis urged that Austin remove all confusion by issuing a specific call, naming the place and indicating the number of delegates to be sent from each municipality.

But before Austin received these suggestions, a new crisis appeared as a result of a renewal of activities on the part of the Mexican military officials. Early in September, Ugartechea had decided that energetic measures should be taken to preserve order in Texas, and information was sent out that Cos was expected to arrive at San Antonio about the middle of the month with the intention of making an immediate attack on the Anglo-American settlements. At the same time, Cos sent word that the individuals whose arrest had been demanded must be surrendered, and that the people of Texas must submit unconditionally to any reforms that the national congress might make in the constitution of 1824. In a circular letter of September 19, therefore, Austin informed the people that further attempts at "conciliatory measures with General Cos and the military at San Antonio are hopeless, and that nothing but *ruin* to Texas can be expected from any such measures. . . . War is our only resource. There is no other remedy but to defend our rights, our country, and ourselves by force of arms." Two days later he reported the receipt of positive information that Cos had landed at Copano with supplies and was awaiting the arrival of four hundred troops, and he stated that a call had been sent out for volunteers to meet at a designated point on the Colorado River on September 28 to oppose Cos's advance. In the face of these developments the previous stand on the organization of local government was abandoned, and Austin now took the position that the consultation must "organize a system of defense and give organization to the country so as to produce concert," because, he said, "until some competent authority is established to *direct,* all that can be done is to recommend." He insisted that there must be "no half way measures," but "war in full," and added that he was going into this war "cheerfully and with very different feelings from what I had in any of our past difficulties," because the Texans were now defending their rights against military usurpation, and the justice of their action would be acknowledged "by an impartial world."

From this point developments were rapid. Austin distributed the news as speedily as possible to all parts of the province and urged immediate mobilization. The response was prompt. Within a week armed men from the nearer settlements were moving individually and in groups toward the appointed meeting place. Although the election for delegates to the consultation had been set for October 5, the polls were opened earlier so that the volunteers might cast their votes before leaving home. It was suggested that militia companies should be organized to ensure a reserve force. Plans were begun for obtaining supplies for the proposed advance. Detailed reports concerning the quantity of arms and ammunition in the various communities were sent to the San Felipe committee. In short, the same Texans who had spent the last three months in trying to avoid war because they could not understand the confused state of affairs were now proceeding boldly into that war under the inspiration of the one man whose influence had done most to foster the desire for peace. Perhaps the surest proof of Austin's greatness as a leader was the fact that within a month after his return to Texas the issues had been clarified, distrust and bitter factionalism had been allayed, and public opinion had been consolidated in support of the same issues that had so recently led to dissension. Thus the consultation which was to meet on October 15 had to face, not the task of uniting the people upon a single line of action —the purpose for which it had been called—but that of providing the necessary organization for carrying out a decision which had already been made.

III

THE STRUGGLE FOR THE
FEDERAL CONSTITUTION

WITH TEXAN volunteers gathering on the Colorado at the same time that additional Mexican troops were being landed at Copano, both sides at last realized that open hostilities could no longer be averted, though neither side was able to understand the full import of the conflict toward which they were advancing. The immediate issue was the Mexican plan to use military force for the purpose of restoring order in Texas, while the Texans were convinced that if they were given the chance they could maintain order for themselves. But the situation was complicated by the belief of the Texans that they were to be deprived of rights and privileges which they thought had been guaranteed them by the constitution of 1824. For them, therefore, the coming of the Mexican troops implied that unless they were willing to submit to centralized authority exercised through military despotism, they must defend the federal system of government.

On the Mexican side the mere matter of governmental form was less important than national pride. The Texans must be convinced that orders from Mexican officials could not be disregarded with impunity, and the realization that previous efforts to accomplish this had proved abortive apparently increased the determination to ensure the success of this attempt by adopting vigorous measures. The general issue, therefore, was that of deciding the relation between national authority and local privilege. But underlying this was the mutual feeling of racial distrust which had played such an important part throughout the whole colonial period. Had the past relations of these two groups not been enveloped in such an atmosphere, the Mexican authorities might not have thought it necessary to insist so drastically on unequivocal submission, or the Texans might not have believed so firmly that submission would endanger their liberty. As the situation stood, however, the Texans could recall unpleasant experiences with other Mexican troops in 1832, and they could also prove that Santa Anna had already destroyed the local privileges of other parts of the Mexican republic. Hence they were willing to accept Austin's statement that "War is our only resource."

But without an authorized agency to direct their organization and movements, without previous experience in concerted action, and even without a complete understanding of what they were expected to do, the Texans were in no sense ready to begin effective military operations. The call for volunteers to intercept Cos's advance had been unofficial, and before it could be endorsed by Austin, individuals and groups were already on their way to the appointed rendezvous. The spontaneity of the response threatened to leave some of the settlements entirely unprotected against possible attacks by Indians or Mexicans, and apparently few of the volunteers stopped to consider the rashness of attempting to oppose a veteran force under an experienced general with an undisciplined, unorganized group of frontiersmen without a commander and without the essential equipment for a campaign.

On the other hand, their courage, initiative, and resourcefulness, combined with their determination to resist oppression and to maintain their rights, gave them a self-confidence that inevitably begot an enthusiasm which no Mexican mind could comprehend. But because of the lack of organization their attention was easily diverted from Cos when Ugartechea ordered the inhabitants of Gonzales to give up a cannon which had been in their possession for four years for use in defending themselves against Indian attacks. Convinced that this demand was for the sole purpose of disarming the Anglo-Americans, the local officials refused to obey and began to prepare for the defense of the town. An appeal for assistance was sent to the other communities, and the volunteers at once changed their objective from the Colorado to the Guadalupe. It was here that the opening clash of arms took place, when on the morning of October 2 the Texans attacked and routed the Mexican force which had been sent to obtain the cannon.

Fully aware that through this action resistance had become an accomplished fact, the Texans now turned their attention to securing a vigorous continuation of the campaign in order to forestall the possibility of an aggressive move on the part of the main Mexican force. Austin immediately issued a circular address "to state as briefly as possible the leading facts which have given rise to this excitement," in which he emphasized the destruction of the federal constitution and declared that the people must either submit or prepare for defense, because, he said, "it is the intention of the Mexicans to march into the colonies, and regulate the land affairs and a great many other things by military force; also, to clear the country of what they choose to call vagrants." In a letter urging the people of Nacogdoches to join the army already in the field, he said: "But one spirit, one common purpose animates every one in this department, which is to take San Antonio and drive all the military out of Texas before the campaign closes."

In the meantime volunteers continued to arrive at Gonzales, and Cos took advantage of their inadvertence by completing his march to San Antonio without interference. When he announced that he was now ready to advance "with a force of every description of arms, sufficient to prove that the Mexicans can never suffer themselves to be insulted," Austin joined the volunteers and was immediately elected by them to serve as their commander. On learning that a small group of Texans had captured the Mexican outpost at Goliad and thus had cut the line of communications between San Antonio and the nearest port through which Cos might receive supplies and reinforcements, he decided to move at once against the main force of the enemy; and on October 12 the army began the march toward San Antonio, imbued with the belief that "twenty days will be apt to close the military career of Cos in Texas."

But the experiences of the next three weeks brought disillusionment. The looseness of the organization made it difficult to submerge the individualistic spirit of the men, and when the commander in chief sought to impress upon them the importance of order and discipline, he felt constrained to assure them that he was not trying to interfere with their individual liberty. Since there was no regular enlistment and no oath, the men felt free to withdraw at will, and they sometimes left in squads. Adequate supplies were at no time available, and Austin complained that cannon were sent without the necessary ammunition; that despite the scarcity of food for both men and horses, he was forced to take stringent measures to prevent its reckless waste; and that the men needed blankets, shoes, clothing, and medicines. After several fruitless suggestions that liquors were not desired, he finally exclaimed: "In the name of Almighty God send no more ardent spirits to this camp—if any is on the road turn it back, or have the head knocked out." When after nine days of desultory marching this force reached Salado Creek, five miles from San Antonio, it was more like a mob than an army, and the credit for keeping it together at all should unquestionably go to Austin's patience and pertinacity. It was in no condition, however, to undertake an assault, and it settled down to a somewhat ineffective siege of the Mexican position, while some of its officers and men began to insist that it should never have left Gonzales.

Most of this confusion was due to the fact that the Texans had been precipitated into military activities before they could complete their plans for holding the general consultation. Until this body could meet and provide for some form of governmental machinery, there was no authorized agency which could act for all parts of the country. But the election of delegates did not take place until three days after the opening fight at Gonzales, and when the time arrived for beginning their sessions, many of the men who had been elected were with the army on its march to San Antonio. Austin had foreseen this contingency and had recommended that each committee of safety send a representative to San Felipe to co-operate with the committee of that place in forming a provisional organization which might assume the direction of affairs until the meeting of the consultation. Only two communities responded, but their representatives joined the two remaining members of the San Felipe committee in forming what they called "the permanent council." For a short time this group merely continued the work that Austin had been doing in spreading information, but its membership as well as its activities increased on October 16, the date set for the meeting of the consultation, when thirty-two of the eighty-four elected delegates assembled at San Felipe. Because of the lack of a quorum this group adjourned until November 1, after resolving that all who could do so should join the army, while those who could not were invited to affiliate themselves with the permanent council.

Nineteen members were present at the council meeting on October 17, and on the following day they issued an address to the people, explaining that since "Texas is without a head this council has been formed to act as one until the general consultation can be held." From this time until it was absorbed into the consultation, this body not only worked feverishly to provide the army with adequate supplies and equipment but it also assumed the responsibility of inaugurating a permanent policy by taking action on such important matters as the establishment of a postal system, the organization of a force of rangers for defense against Indians, the closing of all land offices and the suspension of surveys, the issuing of letters of marque and reprisal, the confiscation of public funds which were in the hands of local agents of the Mexican government, the formulation of an appeal to the people of the United States for aid, and the appointment of an agent who was authorized to "pledge the public faith, the public domain, or both" in return for a loan of one hundred thousand dollars. Because of its unofficial character and its lack of power to enforce its provisions, however, it did not receive the wholehearted support of the people; hence little of its work could be considered as final. Its most important contribution was the fact that it furnished a medium for the dissemination of information concerning the existing state of affairs, while it should also be given credit for the gathering and forwarding of such supplies as reached the army during this period.

Meanwhile the failure to secure a quorum for the consultation not only had postponed the beginning of authorized and representative action in the conduct of the revolution but also had furnished ample cause for anxiety concerning the possibility of securing such action. In accordance with the plan which had finally been adopted, elections had been held in twelve municipalities; but delegates from only eight of these appeared at San Felipe on October 16 for the opening session, while no district had a full representation present. Faced with the necessity of two weeks of inactive waiting, the members became restless; and there was danger that they would disperse before

November 1, thus destroying the chances of completing the organization at that time. But the situation was saved, so far as most of them were concerned, by giving them the opportunity to join the permanent council. For those members who had gone to the army, however, another serious problem arose. When they began preparations to return for the meeting of November 1, their companions refused to let them go, and it was only after Austin and others had explained the urgent necessity of holding the consultation that the excitement subsided sufficiently to permit a vote on the question. A settlement was reached through the decision of the army that all delegates who were not staff officers should be allowed to leave. Unfortunately this decision deprived the consultation of the services of such men as Austin, Travis, and Wharton, who had played leading parts in bringing it into existence.

At the same time, questions were being raised concerning the amount of power which had been delegated to the consultation, and attention was being called to the fact that it was supposed to investigate conditions and report back to the people with recommendations rather than undertake to make any important changes in the existing system. Austin had already sought to prevent drastic action by drawing up a program of what he thought should be done, and his suggestions were made the basis of the address in which Branch T. Archer, on accepting the presidency of the consultation, outlined the general course to be followed. This plan recommended that the consultation should begin its work by issuing a statement of the causes which had impelled the Texans to take up arms; that a provisional government should be established; and that necessary steps should be taken toward the organization of a more adequate military force, the raising of funds, and the adjustment of land problems. But when the attempt was made to follow these suggestions it at once became evident that before a declaration of causes for taking up arms could be formulated it was necessary to determine whether they were fighting for independence or in defense of the constitution of 1824. Many of those who had belonged to the original war party were now advocating a complete separation from Mexico; but Austin's influence was being exerted in behalf of adherence to the federal constitution, and supporting him were members of the former peace party, who, although they accepted the war, were still essentially conservative in their attitude.

After three days of discussion, in which, according to an observer, "coolness and moderation pervaded throughout the debate," it was decided by a vote of 33 to 15 not to declare for independence, and a committee of twelve was instructed to draw up a statement of causes based upon the principles of the constitution of 1824. The report presented by this committee on November 7 represented an attempt to satisfy the demands of both sides, with the result that it was later characterized by Austin as tending fully as much to independence as to adherence to the constitution. After a preamble charging Santa Anna with having overthrown the federal institutions of Mexico, thus dissolving "the social compact which existed between Texas and the other members of the Mexican confederacy," the declaration stated that the people of Texas had taken up arms "in defence of their rights and liberties, which were threatened by the encroachments of military despots, and in defence of the republican principles of the federal constitution of Mexico." It repudiated the right of "the present authorities of the nominal Mexican republic" to govern in Texas and, "stimulated by the generosity and sympathy common to a free people," offered support and assistance "to such of the members of the Mexican confederacy as will take up arms against military despotism." But the note of uncertainty was struck in the fifth article, which declared that the people "hold it to be their right during the disorganization of the federal system, and the reign of despotism, to withdraw from the union, to establish an independent government, or to adopt such measures as they may deem best calculated to protect their rights and liberties, but that they will continue faithful to the Mexican government so long as that nation is governed by the constitution and laws that were formed for the government of the political association."

Although the printed journal merely states that the declaration was unanimously adopted on the morning of November 7, other records show that the rest of the day was spent in discussing it, and on the next day the consultation passed a resolution requiring that it be signed by all members. In fairness to these signers it should be pointed out that the ambiguous character of the declaration was due not so much to a conscious desire to equivocate as to the logic of the situation. While they were aware that the Mexican congress had, in a decree of October 3, annulled the constitution of 1824 by dissolving the constitutional state governments and providing for an administration by officials directly responsible to the central government, they were not sure that the states would submit to this program. The refusal of the majority to approve a declaration of independence, therefore, was based on a hope of a revolution against Santa Anna by those suppressed states, in which case Texas would not have to fight alone. But since unanimity was desirable in order to convey the proper impression, not only to the Mexican liberals but also to the people of Texas, it seemed necessary to make concessions to the persistent demands of the minority.

In fact the difference between the positions of the two factions lay primarily in their inability to agree on the question of methods. Both were determined not to submit to the changes which Santa Anna was carrying out, but the majority doubted the ability of Texas to oppose him singlehandedly, while the minority believed that no aid could be expected from the Mexican liberals. But even while they were advocating cautious measures in order to avoid antagonizing prospective allies, many of the majority realized the possibility of disappointment; thus the minority succeeded in giving the declaration a stronger trend toward independence than its numerical strength warranted, because the logic of the situation was against the adherents of the constitution of 1824. In any event, however, the declaration as adopted went no further than expressly reserving the privilege of taking other steps in case this move did not bring the desired results. But for the time being the implications were perhaps of less significance than the immediate interpretation of the document, and having secured the desired unanimity in adopting it, the majority apparently proceeded to construe it in unequivocal terms. The first evidence of the sincerity of its stand was provided on November 8, when in expressing gratitude to citizens of New Orleans for their offers of assistance the consultation stated that the mouth of the Brazos River "would be the most advisable point to land whatever support our friends may send to enable us to defend the rights guaranteed by the constitution of 1824." It also provided for the translation of the declaration into Spanish "for distribution among our Mexican fellow citizens of the republic," and its good faith was further manifested in connection with the organization of a provisional government, when it required every officer and member of that government to subscribe to an oath to "support the republican principles of the constitution of Mexico of 1824."

The appearance of unanimity quickly vanished, however, when the consultation turned its attention to the organization of a provisional government which might assume responsibility for directing the revolution. It required five days of acrimonious debate, in which two plans were presented and rejected and a third was riddled with amendments, before the delegates could agree upon an ordinance which provided for a governor, who was to "be clothed with full and ample executive powers"; a council, to be composed of one member from each municipality; and a lieutenant governor, who was to be president of the council. The plan specified that the duties of the council should be "to devise ways and means to advise and assist the governor in the discharge of his functions" and to pass only such laws "as in their opinion the emergency of the country requires," but it did not differentiate clearly between executive and legislative authority. Instead of designating the respective provinces of the two branches individually, the ordinance stated, for example, that "the governor and council shall be authorized" to contract loans, to hypothecate the public land as security for their payment, to impose and regulate customs duties, to create and fill such offices as they might deem proper, and to organize, reduce, or increase the military forces as the emergencies seemed to require. In a succeeding article, which was apparently intended to define the work of the governor alone, it was provided that he should be commander in chief of the army and navy, "and he shall have full power, by himself, by and with the consent of the council, and by his proper commander, to direct the military activities of the country, for which purpose he shall be clothed with all these and all other powers which may be thought necessary by the permanent council." Later developments soon showed that not even its authors were sure what this provision meant.

The document had obviously been put together in haste, and as a result it reflected accurately the confusion which existed in the minds of its framers. Failure to define the terms which were being used, combined with looseness of organization and lack of precision in expression, made it almost certain that conflict would arise between the governor and the council as the plan was put into operation. The consultation as a whole elected Henry Smith to serve as governor and James W. Robinson as lieutenant governor, while the individual delegation from each municipality chose one of its own number to represent the municipality as a member of the council. The fact that Smith had been an active advocate of independence and that a majority of the council members favored continued adherence to the constitution of 1824 increased the probability of friction, and it soon became apparent that the two branches of government were in disagreement not only in the matter of division of authority but also in their conception of the real aim of the revolutionary movement which they were expected to direct.

When the provisional government began its work on November 14, Governor Smith addressed his opening message to "the Legislative Council" and referred to himself as "the Supreme Executive," thus implying a definite separation of powers. Acting upon this implication, the council passed an ordinance regulating the method of procedure in legislation, in which the power of veto was conferred upon the governor. Smith immediately vetoed this measure and the council sustained his objections. Having thus established the fact that the veto power was inherent in his office, the governor proceeded to exercise it rather freely. He quarreled with the council over almost every conceivable subject from the filling of petty offices to the formulation of plans for organizing and supporting the army, and after the first two weeks it seemed that the usual procedure was to become the adoption of an ordinance by the council, its veto by the governor, and its passage over the veto.

The most serious aspects of the conflict centered around the question of the military organization and operations, and here too the basis for confusion seems to have been provided in the action of the consultation. Early in its sessions that body had recognized the existence of the volunteer army by assuming responsibility for its expenses, and it had then provided for the enrollment of all able-bodied men into militia companies and for the creation of a regular army of 1,120 men, to be enlisted for two-year terms under the command of a major general who was to be appointed by the consultation, commissioned by the governor, and subject to the orders of the governor and council. For this position Sam Houston, one of its own members, was chosen by acclamation, after which the consultation proceeded to adopt a resolution to the effect that since the army then in the field "is composed of volunteers from every rank of citizens in the country, whose services generally commenced before the assembling of this house, and as their movements have hitherto been regulated by officers of their own choice, no obligation can be imposed upon them to submit to the control of the provisional government; advisory communications are all that can be made to them."

Thus Texas had one army on paper and another army in the field, with the anomalous situation that only the paper army was subject to the direction of the government. And it soon became apparent that various interests were not in complete accord as to where the emphasis should be placed in military mat-

ters. In his first message to the council Governor
Smith urged haste in the organization of the militia.
The council, on the other hand, felt that its first duty
was to sustain the volunteer army already in the field.
Houston insisted that these volunteers should be with-
drawn from their position before San Antonio and
furloughed and that immediate attention should be
given to the organization of the regular army. Obviously, not all of these plans could be carried out at
once, and for the time being the council had the advantage. On November 15 it voted unanimously to
encourage the volunteers to maintain their siege, and
during the next three weeks strenuous efforts were
made to forward provisions, equipment, and clothing
to this army, while urgent calls were sent out for
additional volunteers to join it for an effective attack
on San Antonio.

By the beginning of December bitter criticism from
both Smith and Houston was being met with equally
bitter recriminations from the council, when the development of a crisis in the situation at San Antonio
drew the attention of the country as a whole to the activities of the volunteer army. Throughout the early
part of November, Austin had continued his valiant
struggle to maintain a semblance of order in the force
under his command, and almost no fighting had been

done. He was recalled by the consultation, however, to go on a mission to the United States, and on taking his leave of the army on November 24 he called for volunteers who would pledge themselves to continue the siege under a commander of their own choice. The 405 men who agreed to remain at once elected Edward Burleson as commander, and for the next few days an effort was made to bombard the Mexican position, in which the Texans were reduced to using the cannon balls that had been shot at them by the enemy. A crisis came when on December 3 a majority of the officers voted, over Burleson's objection, to raise the siege and retire to Goliad or Gonzales. But when arrangements were begun the next day to carry out this decision, the opponents of the move took matters into their own hands and called for volunteers to storm the town. About 250 men responded, and after five days of house-to-house fighting General Cos surrendered on December 11 and was permitted to withdraw his army from Texas.

Meanwhile the council, still unaware of these developments at San Antonio, had at last begun the appointment of regimental officers for the regular army. Its proceedings were interrupted, however, when on December 9 a messenger from Burleson brought news of the beginning of the assault and an urgent appeal for ammunition and reinforcements. Impelled by a sense of impending disaster, the council immediately completed the roster of officers from colonels down to third lieutenants and appropriated forty thousand dollars (which it did not have) for the expenses of the army. Houston issued a stirring call for enlistments, but those Texans who were willing to fight were either already in the volunteer army or on their way to it; and as a result the regular army now consisted of a complete staff of officers for ten companies of infantry, ten of artillery, and six of cavalry, with no men for them to command.

The successful campaign against San Antonio had been carried on almost entirely by Texan volunteers, and within a few days after Cos's surrender most of these men, including their commanding officer, left for their homes, on the assumption that the war was over. The council adopted a resolution encouraging this action, while the governor ordered Houston to take charge at San Antonio; but the contingent which remained in camp, consisting largely of newly arrived volunteers from the United States, elected Frank W. Johnson as their commander and announced that they would not take orders from the officers of the regular army. Johnson, signing himself as "Commander-in-chief of the Federal Volunteer Army of Texas,"

wrote to the provisional government that Santa Anna
was planning a new invasion of Texas and urged that
the frontier outposts be strengthened; and the council
at once proposed that an active campaign should be
begun as soon as possible with a view to taking
Matamoros, near the mouth of the Rio Grande, before the Mexicans had time to fortify the place.

While this shift from a defensive to an offensive
plan of action was undoubtedly due partly to a desire
to keep the newly arrived volunteers occupied, it was
primarily the natural outcome of the belief of the conservative leaders that co-operation with the liberal
faction in Mexico in defense of the constitution of
1824 was still possible. Following the adoption of the
declaration of causes for taking up arms numerous
suggestions had been made for the organization of an
expedition under some prominent Mexican liberal to
establish contact with the opponents of Santa Anna
in the northeastern section of Mexico, but Governor
Smith's unconcealed distrust of all Mexicans had thus
far effectively checked the efforts to carry out such
plans. Now, however, the council seemed determined
to override his objections, and although on January 5
it authorized Johnson to undertake the proposed expedition, the opposition of the governor apparently
caused him to hesitate. Impatient for action, the

council then named James W. Fannin to take command; and when Johnson reconsidered a day later, his authorization was confirmed while Fannin's was not recalled. Both men at once issued proclamations calling for volunteers, which caused Houston to protest bitterly that these activities undermined his position as commander of the regular army.

But the most violent reaction came from the governor. On receiving a complaint that Johnson had appropriated the entire stock of movable supplies and equipment at San Antonio for the use of his expedition, he flew into a rage. Calling the members of the council into a special session on Sunday, January 10, he sent them a message in which they were denounced as Judases, scoundrels, wolves, and parricides and were told that unless they rescinded the authorizations for the Matamoros expedition by noon of the next day, they should consider themselves adjourned. The council responded by branding the charges as "false and unfounded," condemning the language as "low, blackguardly and vindictive, and disgraceful to the office from which it emanated," and denying that the governor had the authority to terminate its sessions without its consent. It then voted to suspend Smith from office and to bring impeachment charges against him, and it administered the oath of office to

Lieutenant Governor Robinson to serve as acting governor. From this point each side refused to recognize the other, and hopeless confusion developed as both Smith and Robinson undertook to direct public affairs. The council itself, unable to muster a quorum after January 17, made an ineffectual attempt to continue its work through an advisory committee, but for the next six weeks Texas was virtually without a government.

The effect of this situation on the military operations was of course disastrous. As the plans for the Matamoros expedition continued, Fannin succeeded in raising over four hundred men, largely from the volunteers who came into Texas from the United States during January, and with this force he settled down at Goliad to await developments. Johnson established his headquarters at Refugio, with a force composed mostly of volunteers from the United States who had reached San Antonio in December. Houston, representing the authority of the governor, went about making speeches to the volunteers, in which he declared that the Matamoros expedition was unauthorized and unwise, and he managed to persuade most of Johnson's men to give up the enterprise. In the meantime Colonel James C. Neill, who had been left in command at San Antonio, appealed for reinforcements and Houston sent James Bowie, who did not hold a commission in the regular army, with a small force to dismantle the fortifications there and to remove the artillery. At the same time, Governor Smith ordered William B. Travis to reinforce the post with thirty men who had enlisted in the regular army; and when Neill withdrew soon after Travis' arrival, the volunteers under Bowie refused to accept Travis as their commander. Thus the military organization was following rapidly the path toward disintegration that had already been taken by the provisional government. Houston abandoned his efforts to recruit men for the regular army and went off to eastern Texas to negotiate a treaty with the Cherokee Indians. The Matamoros expedition had been broken up, and any chance that it might have offered to divert the war from Texas through co-operation with the Mexican liberals had been dissipated. Each commander was now left to work out his own plans in the face of a new Mexican advance, and because of the lack of concerted action the frontier outposts were neither abandoned nor adequately protected.

It was just as this disorganization had destroyed all possibility of efficient military operations that the long-threatened Mexican invasion swept in on the unprepared Texans. By the middle of February a

Mexican army of approximately six thousand men had crossed the Rio Grande in accordance with plans that had been maturing for at least three months for the purpose of crushing the rebellion in Texas. The main force, commanded by Santa Anna himself, reached San Antonio on February 23 and began the famous siege of the Alamo. The right wing, under General José Urrea, advanced by way of Matamoros and on February 27 surprised and annihilated a small detachment of Johnson's diminished force at San Patricio. On March 2 the remainder of this force was also destroyed, and the Mexicans then proceeded toward Fannin's position at Goliad. In rapid succession there followed the desperate defense and heroic sacrifice at the Alamo on March 6, the occupation of Refugio by Urrea on March 14, and the defeat and capture of Fannin's force on March 19 and 20, to be followed a week later by the massacre of the prisoners.

The details of this tragic series of disasters are too well known to require recapitulation here, but certain aspects seem to call for special consideration. Perhaps the most striking concrete illustration of the confused state of affairs is to be found in the fact that Travis, who held a commission as colonel of cavalry in the regular army, died defending a fort against

Mexican assaults, and Johnson, who had been appointed major of artillery, was surprised far out on
the frontier in charge of a cavalry unit which had
refused to join the regular army, while Fannin, who
was officially the commander of the proposed artillery
regiment, was at the head of a volunteer infantry
force at the time of his surrender. But this malad-
justment does not explain the tragedy which came to
the Texan arms. Instead it was merely a symptom of
a more fundamental disorder, the cause for which
has to be found in the anarchy resulting from the
inability of too many minor leaders to subordinate
their own selfish aims, individual prejudices, factional intrigues, and personal jealousies and ambitions
to the common good. Possibly it took Goliad and the
Alamo to shock the Texans into a realization of the
need for concerted action.

More significant, however, is the fact that the
destruction of these forces had little direct effect
upon either the condition of the regular army or the
strength of the resident man power of Texas. Here
it should be recalled that the campaign against San
Antonio had been carried on by Texan volunteers for
the avowed purpose of driving the Mexican troops
out of their province, and that for them this objective
had been accomplished with the surrender of Cos and

the withdrawal of his army across the Rio Grande. As they returned to their homes, they seem to have persuaded themselves that so long as the Mexican government refrained from interfering in their affairs there was no need for further military activities; and they even refused to believe the persistent reports that Santa Anna was planning a new invasion of Texas. Consequently they found it difficult to display any serious interest in the efforts to create a regular army, or to consider the proposed Matamoros expedition as their responsibility. Thus the men who were at the frontier outposts to meet the first impact of the renewed Mexican advance were not Texans, but were champions of Texas who had recently come from the United States. Johnson's force, for example, consisted of the remnants of two companies from New Orleans and one from Mobile which had reached San Antonio just in time to participate in the capture of Cos's army in December. About half of the men who died in the Alamo were recent arrivals from Tennessee, Kentucky, and Alabama. Of the ten companies which fought and surrendered with Fannin, three had been organized in Alabama and supplied with arms from the state arsenal, three in Georgia, and two in Kentucky, while the other two consisted of a few Texans, augmented by immigrant volunteers who had come individually or in small groups. So far as available evidence shows, out of approximately seven hundred men killed in action or massacred as prisoners in these disasters of the spring of 1836, less than one fifth had been residents of Texas at the beginning of hostilities in the fall of 1835.

This fact undoubtedly goes far toward explaining —though it does not excuse—the character of the treatment accorded to these men by the victorious Mexicans. Santa Anna was well aware of the sympathy for the Texan cause which was being manifested in the United States, and at the beginning of his plans for putting down the rebellion he sought to cut Texas off from American aid by issuing a decree that all foreigners who might be caught under arms on Mexican soil should be treated as pirates and shot. However proper this may have been from his point of view, its effect was to confirm the conviction that the Texans were at war to save themselves from military despotism, and to strengthen the determination of Americans to come to their assistance. As these American volunteers left their homes, full of enthusiasm for the Texan cause, they could not foresee that by the time they reached their destination the apathy, mismanagement, and confusion in Texas would place them in a position where they seemed to be continuing a resistance which the Texans themselves had apparently abandoned. Nor could the Mexican leaders have been expected to foresee that when they lined up nearly four hundred prisoners of war to be shot in cold blood, they were laying the basis for a reaction that would ultimately destroy any advantage which their victories had gained. It would be interesting to speculate on a recent suggestion that if these prisoners had been paroled and landed on the wharves at New Orleans, "each with his painful story of Texan mismanagement and neglect, Texas' standing with the American people would have fallen to a new low" and the next stage of the revolutionary conflict would have lost the benefit of American money and men. But since they were executed instead of paroled, such questions will have to be left in the realm of speculation.

So far as the Texans were concerned, however, one of the most important results of these developments was the clarification of the issues on which their opposition to Mexican rule rested. Strictly speaking, they had not thus far been engaged in a revolution against Mexico itself, but according to their own declaration they had taken up arms to defend the federal constitution of 1824 against the threats of

Santa Anna's centralist designs. In other words, from their point of view Santa Anna was the revolutionist. Officially, therefore, they had set up a provisional government for a prospective Mexican state which was trying to prevent him from changing the established order, and their military organization and operations had been for the purpose of resisting his encroachments upon the rights and privileges which they claimed under that order. As long as there was a possibility of similar resistance from the liberal elements in the other parts of the Mexican republic, their position was tenable; but the centralist forces had stamped out the liberal opposition in one Mexican state after another until only the Texans were left to be brought into line. It was now clear that the struggle for the federal constitution was a hopeless cause, and as Santa Anna's army advanced toward their province, the Texans found themselves face to face with the necessity of choosing between complete submission to the changed order in Mexico and the adoption of a new basis for the continuation of their struggle. As is well known, they chose to declare their independence; but as their representatives met to make this decision, the Mexican army wiped out what seemed to be their entire frontier defense and Santa

Anna prepared for a triumphal advance into the heart of the settled area on a campaign of execution, expulsion, and confiscation. For the Texans, therefore, the war had now become a struggle for survival.

IV

INDEPENDENCE AND POLITICAL STABILITY

ALTHOUGH the action of the Texans in adopting a declaration of independence came at the very moment when the outlook for the success of their cause seemed darkest, it would be a mistake to consider it as a sudden act of desperation. Actually, it represented the expression of a sentiment which had been present at the beginning of the conflict in the fall of 1835 and which had been growing in strength as the provisional state government ran its confused and factious course toward self-destruction. It will be recalled that at the insistence of a strong minority in the consultation the declaration of causes for taking up arms included a statement that the right was reserved "to withdraw from the union, to establish an independent government, or to adopt such measures as [may seem] best calculated to protect their rights and liberties." The consultation had adjourned to meet again on March 1, unless called together earlier by the governor and council; but before the provisional government was a month old, the council had succumbed to the pressure of public opinion by passing, over the governor's veto, an ordinance providing for the calling of a convention to supplant the proposed reassembling of the consultation. The election of delegates was to be held on February 1, and the new body was to have "ample, unlimited, or plenary powers as to the form of government to be adopted."

During the six weeks between the adoption of the ordinance and the holding of the election the developments in Texas had begun to indicate the approach of a turning point in the course of the revolution. It was becoming increasingly apparent, for example, that there was no longer a possibility of assistance from the Mexican liberals in defense of the federal constitution; and the people, convinced that they must look elsewhere for aid in fighting their battles, began an insistent demand for complete separation from Mexico. Indeed, the citizens of Goliad had boldly proclaimed their position on December 20 by drawing up an indictment of the conduct of both civil and military affairs and concluding with a formal declaration of independence from Mexican rule. Although no other communities were ready to follow this example, no official voice of condemnation seems to have been raised against it; and by the middle of January the last hope of the conservatives was shattered when word came from Stephen F. Austin, who was in the United States on an official mission to obtain assistance for Texas, that in his opinion complete independence was now the goal toward which to work.

Thus the delegates who had been elected on February 1 were fully aware as they assembled for the opening session of the convention on March 1 that they were expected to abandon the original basis of the revolution and to set up a new organization which would become a more effective agency for the continuation of the struggle. That their meetings would have to be held to the accompaniment of military disaster on the frontier had not been foreseen at the time of their election, but the determination with which they completed their task, as well as the character of the work which they did in the midst of a crisis, serves as evidence of their ability, courage, and integrity. Their first act after completing their organization was the appointment of a committee of five to draft a declaration of independence, and the report of this committee, enumerating fourteen specific grievances against Mexico and declaring Texas to be a free, sovereign, and independent republic, was unanimously adopted on the following day. They immediately named a committee to draw up a constitution for the new republic, and during the next few days, while waiting for this committee to report, they assumed the responsibility of a governing agency by turning their attention to numerous matters which had been left undone because of the disintegration of the preceding government. After declining to make a decision on the quarrel between the governor and the council, they provided for a committee to plan a more efficient organization of the physical forces of the country, one to investigate the activities of the land offices, and another to devise a suitable flag for the new nation. On March 4, after an extended discussion, Sam Houston was appointed commander in chief of all the land forces of Texas and was instructed to take command at once and to organize his army. Upon the receipt of Travis' last appeal from the Alamo on the morning of March 6, he withdrew from the convention to assume his new duties, and on the same day an effort to bring about an immediate adjournment to permit the other members to go to the army was defeated by a narrow margin.

The report of the committee on the drafting of a constitution was presented on March 9, and from that time until the early morning hours of March 17 the attention of the delegates was centered on the discussion of the proposed document. This deliberation was made increasingly difficult, however, by the news of the fall of the Alamo and the growing sense of impending disaster as it became known that Houston had ordered the army to withdraw from its positions at Gonzales and Goliad. On the evening of March 16 a hastily convened session undertook to complete the constitution, and shortly after midnight it was adopted with such revisions as had been agreed upon during the course of the earlier discussions. But since the ordinance under which this action was being taken had specified that no constitution which might be formed should be put into effect until approved by a majority vote of the people, it became necessary to provide for a temporary governmental organization to assume the direction of affairs until an election could be held. Accordingly, an ordinance was hurriedly adopted for the establishment of an ad interim government consisting of a president, a vice-president, secretaries of state, treasury, war, and navy, and an attorney general. About four o'clock on the morning of March 17 the convention elected David G. Burnet to the office of president and six of its own members to fill the other offices which it had created. It then delayed adjournment only long enough to clear up a few routine matters, and its members either went directly to the army or hurried home to prepare for the threatened Mexican advance.

The ad interim government at once took over the direction of affairs under conditions that were anything but enviable. It was expressly prohibited from performing either legislative or judicial functions, and as it undertook to act in an executive capacity it found that the only regulations to which it could turn were those adopted by the discredited governor and council, plus the few ordinances that had been enacted by the convention. It had no means of raising revenue and no authority to issue treasury notes, but it was expected to appropriate public funds for use in the defense of the country, to provide men and supplies for the army, and to promote the development of a navy. It was empowered to negotiate treaties with foreign powers and to float a loan of not over one million dollars, for which only the good faith of the country and the hypothecation of the public lands could be offered as security. Such requirements and limitations would have presented serious problems under the most favorable circumstances, but in this case the difficulties were vastly increased by the inexperience of the men who were trying to act and the urgency of the situation in which they were acting.

With the frontier outposts overrun and the victorious Mexican army poised for an advance into the settled area, it was clear that the first problem to be faced was that of self-defense. Having obtained assurance of undivided authority in command, General Houston had gone to Gonzales, where he found an unorganized and undisciplined group of men whom he hoped to use as a nucleus for his army. But before he could mature his plans, the news of the fall of the Alamo and the surrender at Goliad forced him to abandon all thought of an offensive movement, and instead of advancing he began the famous retreat which "continued, with various deflections and pauses, for nearly six weeks, gradually converging toward the coast, and finally coming to an end on the San Jacinto, not far from the eastern border of the settlements."

Meanwhile the convention had provided for the organization and enlistment of the militia, and Houston's army was soon augmented to about twelve hundred men. But as the retreat continued, leaving the settlements defenseless before the Mexican advance, the stories of the atrocities committed at the Alamo and Goliad spread panic among the people, and Texas quickly became a moving mass of fugitives, headed eastward toward the Sabine River and the safety of the United States. Many of the men in the army, becoming desperate, left to aid their fleeing families, while those who remained became insubordinate and sought to force their commander to fight. The ad interim government attempted to allay the panic by issuing reassuring proclamations, only to have the effect destroyed because of its own necessity of seeking safety by moving the seat of government to Galveston Island. It became bitter in its criticism of Houston's strategy and sent the secretary of war to the army to try to bring on a battle. But Houston continued to keep his plans so completely to himself that it is not possible, even now, to determine whether the campaign was being conducted according to a definite plan or whether the meeting of the two armies at San Jacinto was purely accidental. Of the results of the battle, however, there could not be the slightest doubt. The Texans had ended six weeks of retreat with less than thirty minutes of actual fighting, in which the entire advance division of the Mexican army was either killed or captured; and among the prisoners was General Santa Anna himself, who immediately ordered the other divisions of his army to withdraw to Victoria and San Antonio.

While this decisive victory relieved the tension under which the ad interim government had been working, the capture of Santa Anna brought up new problems which in the end threatened to wreck the civil authority. An immediate demand that he be executed in retaliation for the massacre of the Goliad prisoners was checked by Houston's refusal to turn him over to the army; and the government, believing that he might be useful in assuring a cessation of hostilities, proceeded to discuss peace terms with him. The preliminary agreements he had made with General Houston were incorporated into the treaty of Velasco, in which it was specified that the Mexican forces would evacuate the territory of Texas, retiring across the Rio Grande; that they would release all prisoners and restore all private property that had been captured; that they would respect all property rights in their retreat; that a treaty of amity and limits would be concluded, in which the territory of Texas should not be extended beyond the Rio Grande; and that the government of Texas would provide for the immediate embarkation of Santa Anna for Vera Cruz, in order that he might arrange for an official recognition of Texan independence.

Despite the fact that there might have been ample reason to question the validity of a treaty made with a prisoner of war who had not consulted his government, it is obvious from the records that the Texan authorities entered into this agreement in good faith and made every possible effort to carry it out. On the Mexican side, General Vicente Filisola, who had succeeded to the command, seems also to have made an earnest effort to comply with the terms of the agreement, although he felt that the national honor of Mexico had been compromised and that the campaign should be continued. The Texans could not afford to disband their army, however, as long as the Mexicans were still within their territory; but the problem of keeping it together and under control was made especially difficult by the conviction of the average Texan soldier that the war was over and that he ought to be permitted to return to his home as quickly as possible to resume the planting of his crops and begin the rehabilitation of the area which had been devastated in the recent campaign. More than two thirds of the men who fought under Houston at San Jacinto were old residents, and this force apparently began to break up immediately after the battle. Many individuals left without waiting to be discharged, while the mustering out of companies was begun within ten days, and by the middle of May only about three hundred men remained to follow at a distance the course of the Mexican retreat.

The problem of control was increased by the fact

that Houston had been wounded at San Jacinto and had gone to New Orleans early in May for medical treatment. He had suddenly become the idol of the army, and when Thomas J. Rusk was appointed to the command, the men received him with the understanding that he was merely substituting until Houston could return. Rusk had no confidence in the promises of Santa Anna and no sympathy with the arrangement by which the Texans were required to avoid collision with the retreating Mexican troops; and to him it seemed imperative that his dwindling force should be strengthened and provided with adequate supplies for the continuation of its operations. Unable to appreciate the destitute condition of the country as a whole or to realize that the provisional government was swamped with other urgent problems, he construed its failure to respond as willful neglect. His unrestrained criticism apparently encouraged a group of officers in the army to prepare a formal protest, in which they threatened that unless their demands were promptly met they would come to the seat of government to protect their "most sacred rights."

But by the time this threat reached the government, it was already facing a more serious crisis which had developed in connection with the agreement to send

General Santa Anna back to Mexico. On June 1, following two weeks of acrimonious discussion in which two members resigned in protest, the government placed him on board a Texan schooner of war to be taken to Vera Cruz; but while the departure of the vessel was being delayed for the preparation of instructions for the commissioners who were to accompany him, General Thomas J. Green arrived with a large force of volunteers who had just come from the United States by way of New Orleans and Galveston. This group expressed its opposition to the release of Santa Anna, and on the morning of June 4 it removed him from the ship and placed him under guard. A turbulent scene followed, in which members of the cabinet sought to prevent this interference; but in the end the newly arrived volunteers won their point, and the government was forced to leave Santa Anna in the hands of the army. As a result, the members of the cabinet suggested that their authority be surrendered to the people. President Burnet resisted this move on the ground that "our abandonment at such a juncture would throw Texas into irretrievable anarchy and confusion," and at the same time he replied to the protest from Rusk's army that "when the civil government of a country is compelled to receive a prescription of its duties from an armed force, that government is, if not virtually dissolved, in great danger of being lost in the blazonry of military misrule." But through his determination and courage the form of civil government was saved, even though the military interests, as expressed by the newly arrived volunteers, for the time being seemed to have established their ascendancy.

The appearance of these newcomers marked the beginning of a transformation in the character and composition of the army, which was to add materially to the difficulties of the provisional government in its efforts to attain stability for Texas. The nature of the change in composition is indicated by the fact that out of the total of approximately 900 Texans who had participated in the battle of San Jacinto, only 196 are shown by the muster rolls to have remained in the army after the end of July. Yet such muster rolls as can be found for July and August contain the records for 53 companies, with a total of 2,503 officers and men. These records show that 39 of these companies, with a total of 1,831 men, had arrived in Texas after the battle of San Jacinto, and that the remaining 14, with a total of 672 men, represented varying assortments of Texans and recent arrivals.

Thus, just as the Mexican invaders were withdrawing from the country, a Texan army, composed largely of men who had defended their homes and their rights, was being replaced by another force, almost three times as large, consisting of men who as yet had neither homes nor rights in Texas to defend. The attention of most of these newcomers had been attracted to Texas by the dramatic stories of the Mexican atrocities at the Alamo and Goliad and by the promises of liberal land bounties made by desperate Texan agents in the United States during the dark days immediately preceding San Jacinto. They had sworn vengeance against the Mexicans, and on reaching Texas they not only were disappointed to find that the fighting was over, but they also were astonished that the Mexican leaders had not been hanged. Many of them later became useful and substantial citizens of Texas, but for the time being, because they lacked understanding of the situation, they were easily persuaded by ambitious or disgruntled leaders that the country needed to be saved from its own rulers. Consequently they proved to be a turbulent and troublesome group. After his clash with them over the proposed release of Santa Anna, President Burnet realized that they constituted a serious threat to the civil authorities, but he was in no position to try to disband them. He immediately informed the

Texan agents in New Orleans that no more volunteers from the United States were needed, and he sought to provide occupation for those who had already arrived by sending them on a campaign against threatening Indian tribes. His orders were ignored, however, at the instigation of Rusk, who showed his inability to understand the situation by ridiculing this policy and by urging Green to join him immediately. By the middle of July, therefore, most of the newcomers had made their way to the army headquarters.

As might have been expected, a new crisis arose almost immediately. As Rusk came under the influence of these new arrivals, the bitterness of his complaints increased, and the government appointed Mirabeau B. Lamar to supersede him as commander. But when Lamar arrived at headquarters, he was informed that his appointment was looked upon as "an unceremonious interference by the cabinet with the affairs of the army," and was overwhelmingly rejected by a vote of the new volunteers. Accepting this verdict, he withdrew, leaving Rusk in command; but some of the officers, unwilling to stop at this point, held an unofficial meeting in which it was decided that the president and cabinet should be arrested and brought to the army for a military trial. The attempt to carry out this plan was thwarted, however, when the citizens at the seat of government, obviously aware of the seriousness of this threat to the civil authority, indicated their determination to uphold the president. But Texas had been brought perilously near to the establishment for itself of the very sort of military domination that the revolution against Mexico had sought to avert.

This conflict was pushed into the background, however, when word came from New Orleans that the Mexican congress had repudiated Santa Anna's agreements and that the campaign against Texas was being renewed. Without taking time to establish the reliability of this report, Burnet at once issued a call for reinforcements, reversed his former instructions concerning the sending of volunteers from the United States, and set machinery in motion to obtain the supplies for which Rusk had been pleading. Although by the beginning of August only the president, the secretary of the treasury, and the secretary of war remained to carry on the work of government, these three did what they could to provide for the army with the limited resources at their command. As additional volunteers arrived from the United States, they were dispatched to headquarters without delay, and Rusk soon found himself in command of a new army which was impatient for action. When the expected Mexican invasion failed to materialize, he joined with Green and other newcomers in urging an attack on Matamoros; and Burnet, seeing an opportunity to divert the attention of the army from further interference in civil affairs, gave the project his endorsement.

In the meantime other steps were being taken to hasten the attainment of political stability. On July 23, President Burnet issued a proclamation for an election to be held on the first Monday in September for the purpose of ratifying the constitution and selecting the officers of government for which that instrument provided. The names of Stephen F. Austin and Henry Smith were immediately proposed as presidential candidates, and the campaign seemed to revolve around conflicts of the period prior to the declaration of independence until Sam Houston changed the emphasis from bygone issues to personalities by letting it be known through the medium of the army that he was back in Texas and willing to serve. Houston received approximately three fourths of all the votes cast, and Lamar found consolation for his failure to supersede Rusk as commander in chief of the army by defeating him for the vice-presidency by a majority of at least ten to one. The vote in favor of the adoption of the constitution was unanimous, and the voters refused by an overwhelming majority to approve a proposal which would have given the power of amendment to the congress. The personnel of the newly elected congress reflected the absence of clearly defined issues in that it included men who had opposed independence along with those who had been leaders in bringing it about, champions of Burnet's handling of the ad interim government along with some of his harshest critics, and some of the oldest settlers in Texas along with several who had arrived since the battle of San Jacinto.

While the interest of the army was still pointed toward the proposed expedition against Matamoros, Burnet planned the final steps in the transition to the constitutional government. Calling the congress into session early in October, he spent two weeks in submitting to it detailed reports on various aspects of the work of the ad interim government; and when, on October 22, he stepped aside to permit the inauguration of Houston as the constitutional president of the independent Republic of Texas, political stability was assured and the revolution officially came to an end.

If the general impression conveyed by this survey is one of confusion, the difficulty may be due as much to the nature of the revolution itself as to the shortcomings of the treatment which it has received. Not even the Texans themselves were able to understand, as Houston assumed office, that within the brief space of twelve months they had gone through a series of developments analogous on a smaller scale to those in which an earlier group of Americans had taken fourteen years to proceed from the Second Continental Congress to the inauguration of President Washington. Perhaps because their struggle was concentrated, it was also complicated and confused, and in order to understand the movement as a whole it becomes necessary to review some of the major problems whose interrelations determined its general character.

On the basic question of purpose, for example, it will be recalled that the revolution began as resistance to the threat of Mexican military interference, continued as an effort to defend the federal constitution of Mexico, and ended as a war for independence. On the problem of governmental organization to promote these aims there were five phases, varying in length from two weeks to seven months. Beginning with the permanent council, which despite its name was never intended to be more than a temporary expedient to meet an emergency, the agency of direction progressed through the consultation, the governor and council, and the convention, to the establishment of the ad interim government as another temporary expedient to prepare the way for the inauguration of a stable political authority. On the problem of military operations the struggle passed through four well-defined stages. In the first of these, a small volunteer army, composed almost entirely of Texans, had driven the Mexican troops from Texas in December, 1835; in the second, a somewhat larger force, consisting mainly of newly arrived volunteers from the United States, had attempted to take the offensive, and because of lack of co-ordination had met with disaster on the Nueces, at the Alamo, and at Goliad in March, 1836; in the third, the Texans had again taken the field to carry on the campaign which culminated at San Jacinto; and in the fourth, another group of volunteers from the United States again turned the attention toward offensive operations, while it also brought a threat from within of military interference in civil affairs.

Each of these three problems, when considered separately, seems to present a relatively simple pattern; but each was only a part of the revolution, and until the three have been woven together into a composite fabric, the total picture cannot be seen. As this is done, it becomes apparent that much of the complexity and confusion of the revolution arose from the fact that the corresponding stages in their respective developments could not be synchronized. In November, 1835, for example, the problem of governmental organization was being worked out on the basis of defense of the constitution of 1824, while the army was operating on the determination to drive the Mexican troops out of Texas. After the fall of San Antonio the military activities centered around the proposed Matamoros expedition, which meant defense of the constitution of 1824, while the government was being broken up because of the disagreement between the supporters of the constitution and the advocates of independence. In March, 1836, the new government was definitely committed to independence, while the military forces were still operating as the army of the Mexican state of Texas. In April, for the first time during the revolution, the army and the government were in accord on the purpose of their struggle, and the victory at San Jacinto was their reward.

But even this analysis represents an oversimplification, because it leaves the impression that the revolution can be explained in terms of military operations and political interests and activities. Actually, these constitute the warp of a pattern for which the woof is provided by a multiplicity of related problems of a more or less special nature and by the personalities and interests of a large number of individuals who had a part in determining its design. The related problems varied all the way from the petty personal question of who should operate a particular ferry to the fundamental one of finding the ways and means to finance the struggle. Since each problem, no matter how small, became one more piece of material to be fitted in, each made its contribution toward the inability to avoid complication. Many of the lights and shades of the picture are to be found in such trivial incidents as the effort of the council to stop the grinding of corn too near its meeting place and its hasty compromise on discovering that if the grinding was stopped its members would have to go dinnerless, or in its reasoned debate over the best means of sending a thousand-dollar bank note to New Orleans to be exchanged for bills of smaller denomination which could be used in Texas. The records are rich in human-interest stories, ranging from humor to pathos, that furnish invaluable clues to the conditions under which the work of the government and the army had to be carried on.

Among the more important problems only a few can be enumerated here. One of the most troublesome was that of organizing and maintaining agencies of local government, in connection with which protests persistently came in concerning the inefficiency, and frequently the venality, of the men appointed, while the officers themselves complained that they were not kept informed concerning the governmental program. Closely related to this was the specter of land speculation, which could not be ignored; and the attempts to close the land offices brought insubordination, bitterness, and the danger of alienating the interests of many influential individuals, both inside and outside Texas. In addition to the military operations against the Mexicans other problems of defense had to be faced. There was always a threat of Indian attacks, which made it necessary to organize a ranger force and interfered with the raising of the regular army. Efforts to protect the coast line through the granting of letters of marque and reprisal brought difficulties over the disposition of the prizes and complications with the United States on questions of maritime law. The creation of a navy, consisting of four small schooners, brought a greater sense of security against possible Mexican attacks by way of the Gulf and provided convoys for the shipment of troops and supplies until the lack of funds to keep the vessels in proper condition terminated their activities.

The problem of obtaining supplies proved endless. At home the people gave generously as long as their own stocks lasted, but when impressment was attempted, they were emphatic in their resentment against the government. In the United States unofficial manifestations of interest took the form of public meetings all the way from New Orleans to New York, in which funds were raised for the purchase of supplies and the equipping of volunteers, but the hazards of shipping made delivery uncertain. Late in January, 1836, for example, of three ships which left New Orleans together, laden with powder, munitions, clothing, and provisions sufficient to supply the army for the proposed Matamoros campaign, two were wrecked on the uncharted bars off the coast of Texas and their entire cargoes lost. In another case a ship which left New York City in November, 1835, with a contingent of two hundred volunteers and a small cargo of supplies, was detained for two months by British authorities at the Bahama Islands on a charge of piracy and did not reach Texas until the middle of March. Innumerable others got through of course, and in many instances, as in the case of the two cannons from Cincinnati which constituted Houston's artillery at San Jacinto, brought much-needed aid at critical times.

By far the most important of these problems, however, was that of financing the revolution. The beginning of the struggle found the Texans without any system of revenue, and although the assertion of a caustic critic that the authorities, having decided that the possible methods of raising money "might all be resolved into taxing, borrowing, begging, selling, robbing, and cheating, determined to try all six" cannot be accepted in its entirety, it suggests the complexity of the problem. Outright donations of money came in from New Orleans, Mobile, Nashville, Cincinnati, New York, and other places in the United States, and in a few instances from Texans themselves. Public funds in the possession of local Mexican officials were confiscated, and any land dues that were paid went into the hands of the Texan authorities. An effort to devise a system of taxation was abandoned on the ground that it would not bring immediate returns, while an elaborate plan for the collection of import and tonnage duties, adopted by the council, seems to have brought nothing more tangible than complaints from Texan merchants until it was annulled by the convention. In the end, loans based on the hypothecation of public lands proved the most fruitful source of income, while the issuance of land scrip to be sold at the rate of fifty cents an acre also brought a small amount of money. On the whole, however, the revolution was fought largely on credit, which was obtained through the activities of a few Texans and more especially through the financial standing of the firm of William Bryan and Company of New Orleans. At the end of the period, the public debt was estimated at $1,250,000, while the amount spent in actual cash is yet to be ascertained. Confusion in the handling of records, misunderstandings with regard to the work of the New Orleans agencies, and controversy over the terms of the loans obtained in New Orleans and New York combined to make this perhaps the most complex and most irritating problem of the entire struggle.

As for the interests and personalities of the designers, the picture is no less confusing, and it seems safe to say that the general aspect of the revolution was not so much the design of a master planner as it was the product of the unplanned combination of a large number of unskilled participants whose conception of aims and methods differed greatly. Whether we look at the military activities or at civil affairs, there is no single individual whose name stands out in a position of leadership through the whole course of the struggle. Instead, we find a succession of men rising and falling as conditions and issues change, but none of them displaying the qualities which would have enabled them to rise above the issues and win the sustained confidence and support of the whole

[126]

public. Partly because of the work of such men and partly in spite of it the progress of the revolution seemed to evoke almost continuous internal strife, centered sometimes around rival personalities, sometimes around disagreements over principles or methods, and almost always growing out of suspicions and misunderstandings. Although their disagreements increased the confusion, each was undoubtedly striving to advance or protect the interests of Texas as he interpreted those interests, and it would be unjust to impugn the sincerity or the patriotism of any of them.

Of the men whose names are now best known in connection with the revolution, Travis and Fannin are remembered because of the way they died rather than for what they accomplished while living. Henry Smith might have had a chance as provisional governor had he possessed a less obstinate temperament and a modicum of executive ability. Burnet's contribution in maintaining the civil authority until the constitutional government could be established deserves more recognition than he received at the time or has been given since. The two men who came nearest to providing constructive leadership were Stephen F. Austin and Sam Houston, but in both cases circumstances seemed to conspire to undermine their usefulness at the times when the outlook was darkest. Austin's contribution was made at the beginning of the struggle by inspiring the organization of the first phase and consolidating public opinion in its support, but the mischance which placed him in command of the army when he should have been in the consultation and then sent him on a mission to the United States when his judicious counsel would have been invaluable at home deprived Texas of the services which he was best qualified to render. Houston, on the other hand, started as an ambitious troublemaker whose activities seemed to create more enemies than friends until he proved his capacity by holding the army together to win the battle of San Jacinto and then capitalized on the result to emerge as the popular hero of the revolution. "Austin and Houston, working together," one writer has said, "could, and would, have avoided practically all of the costly Texan mistakes"; but since they were kept apart, we are forced to relegate this intriguing suggestion to the limbo of historical imponderables.

It is possible also that any attempt to assess the over-all meaning or significance of the revolution will involve us in a consideration of other questions for which definitive answers cannot yet be given. If we start with Barker's carefully reasoned conclusion that the coming of the conflict "was neither the culmination of a deep-laid program of chicanery and greed nor the glorious response of outraged freemen to calculated oppression of tyrants," we may rule out at once the concept of a conspiracy of interests, whether of slave-holders to incorporate Texas into the United States or of land speculators to create an independent government which they might control. Fundamentally it was the result of the difference between the racial and political inheritances of the two groups of people who came into contact with each other on Mexican soil. As typical Anglo-American frontiersmen, the Texans thought in terms of the political and social institutions to which they and their ancestors had been accustomed under a democratic system of government, and they were unable to appreciate the fact that while Mexico had the form its people were not prepared for the substance of such a system. Thus when such leaders as Santa Anna undertook to adjust the application of the system to the political capacity of eight million Mexicans, some thirty thousand Texans protested against the change as an encroachment upon rights and privileges which they understood and knew how to use. Under other conditions a satisfactory compromise might have been reached, but in the prevailing atmosphere of racial distrust mutual concessions were hardly to be expected.

The immediate cause of the revolution, therefore, was the substitution of centralism for federalism in Mexico and the determination of the Mexican authorities to use force rather than reason to compel an unqualified acceptance of the change. It is a significant fact, however, that as this transformation was being put into effect, the Texans were reluctant to believe that it had any serious implications for them until they faced the threat of military interference in the summer of 1835. They were still thinking of themselves as Mexican citizens who were about to be drawn into the sphere of operations of a revolt against the principles of the federal constitution, and they still had confidence in the willingness and the ability of the liberal element in Mexico to overcome that revolt. Thus even as they organized for defense, they declared their adherence to the constitution of 1824 and set up a provisional government for a prospective Mexican state, and it was only when the futility of this position had become unmistakably clear that they finally took the step which made them revolutionists against Mexico itself.

The place of this revolution in the larger historical perspective is too well known to require more than passing mention in conclusion. In a restricted sense it was of course a significant link in the chain of events which conditioned the relations between Mexico and the United States. In a larger sense it was a logical extension of that general revolutionary struggle by which the New World subjects of England and Spain established their independence from their respective mother countries, and as an Anglo-American revolt against Hispanic-American rule it seemed to suggest that the activities which had hitherto been directed against European control were now to be continued as a part of the purely American development. In still another sense it represents a manifestation of the Anglo-American frontier process being worked out under unusual conditions, and it is in this connection that it may hold its greatest significance as a laboratory for further study. It is possible, for example, that because it was essentially an attempt to follow the traditional frontier procedures in a situation which differed from any previous frontier experience, it could provide a study in comparisons which might throw new light on some of the controversial aspects of the frontier hypothesis. It is possible, also, that because of the high degree of concentration, in both time and space, and because of the relatively small number of people engaged, this struggle may offer an unusual opportunity to study individual conduct and motives under conditions of stress and thus to make a contribution toward the establishment of a more adequate basis for acceptable conclusions with regard to psychological factors in historical interpretation. The one thing which can be suggested with assurance is that the last word concerning the meaning or significance of the Texas Revolution has not yet been said.

DATE DUE

DEC 10 '65			
DEC 7			
DEC 7 '66			
NOV 1 8 '67			
DEC 6 '67			
MAY 4 '70			
NOV 1 8 '70			
APR 2 '86			
GAYLORD			PRINTED IN U.S.A.